PUGIN

Augustus Welby Pugin (1812–1852) by L. R. Herbert

Pugin

PHOEBE STANTON

Preface by

NIKOLAUS PEVSNER

A STUDIO BOOK

THE VIKING PRESS · NEW YORK

Published in 1972 in a hardbound and paperbound edition by
The Viking Press, Inc.
625 Madison Avenue, New York 10022

SBN 670–58216–6 (hardbound)
SBN 670–02021–4 (paperbound)

Library of Congress catalog card number: 78–172898

Printed in Great Britain by Jarrold and Sons Ltd, Norwich

Contents

This study of A. Welby Pugin, his art and his place in his time, is intended to provide an introduction to the character and events of his career and an analysis of the development of his practice, his theories of art and architecture and the growth of his capacities and principles as a designer.

The facts have been drawn from the mass of data in Pugin's diaries, letters, drawings, published books, comments made by him and about him in the public press in his lifetime and the evidence offered by his buildings and his achievement in the arts of decoration. Only the critical assumptions are my own.

The quotations from Pugin's letters are extracted from his correspondence with J. R. Bloxam, E. J. Willson, the Earl of Shrewsbury and John Hardman; for permission to use these excerpts I am indebted respectively to the President and Fellows of Magdalen College, Oxford, The Johns Hopkins University, and the John Hardman Studio, Birmingham. The letters of Bishop Briggs and Bishop Baines on the matter of the vestments used at the consecration of St Mary's, Derby, are from the Westminster Diocesan Archives, Archbishop's House, Westminster, by permission of His Eminence Cardinal Heenan. The description of St Giles', Cheadle, is quoted (verbatim) from Vol. XI of *The Letters and Diaries of John Henry Newman* (edited at the Birmingham Oratory by Charles Stephen Dessain and published by Thomas Nelson and Sons).

There are persons whom I wish to thank for their patient attention to my inquiries and their willingness to let me examine and photograph buildings and objects. The descendants of A. Welby Pugin have given me every encouragement and assistance. The courtesy of the present management of the Hardman Studio was first extended to me years ago when it set me in the direction that was to prove fruitful in my search for Pugin documentation. My gratitude to librarians and archivists in Great Britain, Ireland and the United States is too great to detail, but I mention, as typical of the kindness shown me, that of the staffs of the Library and Drawings Collection of the Royal Institute of British Architects, the Victoria and Albert Museum and the British Museum.

Fellowships and grants from the American Council of Learned Societies, the American Philosophical Society and the Chapelbrook Foundation, and a leave of absence given me by The Johns Hopkins University have made possible the time and travel required for my research and photography.

I wish to thank Dr T. S. R. Boase and Mrs Shirley Bury for their continuing enthusiasm for Pugin's work and Pugin studies. My examination of Pugin and his place in the Gothic Revival was begun under the direction of Sir Nikolaus Pevsner, whose generous interest in my work I herewith partially repay.

Phoebe B. Stanton

The Johns Hopkins University
Baltimore, Maryland.
1970

Preface

Listen to Cardinal Newman:

'... Mr. Pugin is a man of genius; I have the greatest admiration of his talents, and willingly acknowledge that Catholics owe him a great debt for what he has done in the revival of Gothic architecture among us. His zeal, his minute diligence, his resources, his invention, his imagination, his sagacity in research, are all of the highest order. It is impossible that any one, not scientifically qualified to judge of his merits, can feel a profounder reverence than I do, for the gift with which it has pleased the Author of all Truth and Beauty to endow him. But he has the great fault of a man of genius, as well as the merit. He is intolerant, and, if I might use a stronger word, a bigot. He sees nothing good in any school of Christian art except that of which he is himself so great an ornament. The Canons of Gothic architecture are to him points of faith, and everyone is a heretic who would venture to question them.'

Newman did. He argued that Gothic architecture never 'prevailed over the *whole* face of the Church', that for example 'the see of St Peter's never was Gothic', that there is no 'uninterrupted tradition of Gothic architecture', that what Pugin pleads for is a revival, and that no such revival can 'exactly suit the living ritual of the nineteenth century', and that the Oratory to which Newman belonged, is 'a birth of the sixteenth century' and hence cannot be represented by 'a cloister or a chapter house'.

Newman argues sensibly. He tries to be fair – had he not, as Mrs Stanton tells us, called Pugin's church at Cheadle 'the most splendid building I ever saw'? Pugin did not argue in this case at all; he swore, he cursed, he condemned: the Oratorians are 'perfectly monstrous, and I give the whole order up for ever ... It is worse than the Socialists.' An Oratory is 'nothing else than a mechanics' institute', and the whole Italian architectural trend is 'nearly as much horror as the principles of Voltaire.'

But one must take Pugin on his own terms, and this is what Mrs Stanton does splendidly. The present book is only an earnest of a much bigger book which we must all hope to get from her soon. She started work on Pugin over twenty years ago. I advised her against Pugin. We have Ferrey – would she be able to get beyond him? My scepticism proved totally wrong. She found about 3000 letters. She found thirteen sketch books and masses more material. She could not work consistently towards the *magnum opus*. There were delays for human causes, there was a growing load of academic duties, there was much else. Still, what we have here is an essay of which every paragraph is worth while. The result is a new assessment.

In connection with this assessment, I want to return to Newman. All his arguments were right, yet emotionally and aesthetically in the end he was wrong, and Pugin was right. Pugin died in 1852, Newman in 1891. So Newman lived to see the Brompton Oratory (by Gribble). We all know it, and few will deny that it is alien. It is Italian and has not become Anglo-Italian as Osborne has, as Scott's and Matthew Digby Wyatt's Foreign Office has.

Pugin instead established a new phase of Victorian Gothic and was universally followed. It is true that in this establishing process the Cambridge Camden Society helped, Scott helped, Ruskin helped. But Pugin laid the foundation. His best book, the *True Principles*, was begun – so we learn from Mrs Stanton – already in 1838. And before its publication in 1841, Pugin had given up the Perpendicular as his source of forms and ensembles and turned to the Middle Pointed or Second Pointed, i.e. the style current in England from Westminster Abbey to the early fourteenth century. Perpendicular he condemned as Erastian, but there must have also been an aesthetic decision there. Perpendicular – see the Houses of Parliament – likes close surface pattern, the Second Pointed has fewer motifs but bolder

8

motifs, and those Pugin now wanted. The preference discussed by Mrs Stanton which from about 1840 he had for asymmetrical grouping, for steeples not at the west end but in other positions, goes with that change.

But Pugin stands for more change than that. To build Gothic is to him a Christian duty and it became a moral duty to men so diverse as Scott and Ruskin. And as it is a duty, it must be fulfilled with earnestness. That saved much English church architecture of the later nineteenth century from the slackness of discipline which one meets so often in secular buildings. Had there not been the true Pugin principles, we would not have the robust Street, the noble Bodley, the refined Pearson. The architectural control and the conscientiousness of the English Gothic Revival has few parallels in other countries. And then, finally, and here Mrs Stanton is especially enlightening, Pugin's principles lent themselves to adaptation in the field of domestic architecture. A building like Alton Castle has a functional informality which was wholly novel. Again, we would not have Scott's *Remarks on Secular and Domestic Architecture* of 1858, if Pugin had not written and built as he did. Ruskin, profoundly dishonest as he was, denied any influence from Pugin. Scott was more honest. He wrote: 'I was awakened from my slumber by the thundering of Pugin's writings.'

Mrs Stanton could say the same and she says it here handsomely.

Nikolaus Pevsner

CHAPTER ONE

Introduction

The singular career of Augustus Welby Pugin – British architect and designer in the decorative arts, architectural theorist and
critic – began in 1835 and ended with his death at the age of
forty in 1852. In those seventeen years, Pugin designed more
than a hundred buildings, wrote eight major books, and
founded a prosperous business in the production of metalwork
and stained glass windows from his own designs. An active
participant in controversy on architectural and religious
matters, he challenged the reigning tastes of England so
effectively, and lived so vivid a life of dedication to his ideas
that his name became synonymous with the revival of the
Gothic style in architecture and decoration.

Pugin's creative life was even shorter than the bald
biographical facts make it appear. He crowded much of his
accomplishment into the years between 1838, when he built his
first church, and 1846, when his health began to fail. Mean-
while the character of his practice had begun to change; his
monopoly of Catholic building ended as other architects began
to work in his manner. Had he lived, Pugin would surely have
passed into another phase of his career, but at the end of 1851
he was incapacitated by physical and mental disease. In
September 1852, he was dead.

In June 1835, when he was twenty-three years of age, Pugin
became a convert to Catholicism. Ever afterward he thought
of himself as a Catholic first and whatever else he was second.
His faith controlled his activities and dictated the social circles
in which he moved and worked. It was reflected in his critical
determinations and in the urgent feeling of religious and artistic
mission that kept him in the ferment in which he thrived.

Pugin is the unusual case of an architect better known for his lively character, his books, and his caustic criticisms of the architectural and social establishments than for his buildings. Had he not been an author he might well have joined the quiet ranks of the early Victorian church architects, his contagious enthusiasm, his eccentricity, and much of his brilliance hidden from his own generation and those that have followed. In the years after his death, Pugin's fame was sustained by the incisive humour and the architectural and social commentary in the two editions of *Contrasts, or a Parallel between the Noble Edifices of the Fourteenth and Fifteenth Centuries and Similar Buildings of the Present Day,* by the clarity and assertiveness of everything he had written, and by the events of his dramatic life. In the twentieth century, his reputation has grown. Pugin has emerged as a pioneer scholar of medieval art and architecture, and as modern architectural ideas have evolved the prescience of his statements in *True Principles* has become apparent.

Whatever people thought of him in his lifetime, and despite the modernity of some of his opinions, Pugin should also be seen as he saw himself. Fortunately we know what he thought, for in the year 1840, on the threshold of an enormously creative time in his life, he declared his artistic intentions to an admiring and learned gentleman who offered encouragement.

You have done me the great honour of terming me the 1st ecclesiastical architect of the age. If this is true I hold the title only as the *scholar and representative of those Glorious Catholic architects who lived in antient days and to whom the merit of all our present performances are in justice to be referred.* I am continually studying and working in their principles. I seek *antiquity* and not *novelty.* I strive to *revive not invent* and when I have done my best and when compared with the puny and meagre abortions of the day I have produced a sturdy effect yet how terribly do my best efforts sink when tested by the scale of antient excellence.

Both sincerity and ardent naïveté saturate this resolution, and Pugin seems already to have experienced the disappointment which was always to shadow his artistic ambitions. His was a hopeless quest. The more scholarly his knowledge of medieval

11

art became, the less was he to be satisfied with what he could accomplish in the cause of its revival. The will to 'revive not invent' meant, furthermore, that he might deprive himself of the pleasures of invention and be led to deprecate, or even to view with alarm, his own achievements in the medieval styles in the nineteenth century. He was to be his own harshest critic, ready enough to explain and defend his works on religious grounds but rarely to do so without apologies if the purity of his Gothic revivalism were questioned. Better than anyone else, Pugin knew where and how far his buildings fell short of his dreams.

Even without his public avowal of Catholicism, his writing, and his quixotic dedication to Gothic revivalism, his artistic abilities alone would have been enough to bring him fame and clients. In addition to being the best and most appealing architectural illustrator of his day, he possessed the gift of total visual recall; he could remember even the smallest details of objects or buildings he had once seen, and draw them with dazzling rapidity and spontaneity. Had visual memory been his only talent it might have been a curiosity, even a disability, rather than a blessing, but Pugin placed it at the service of his gift as a critic. He spent time and energy on seeking to understand and explain his artistic preferences, and it was his keenness of observation and imitative skill that gave his satirical illustrations and writing their energy and freshness.

Pugin was destined to have difficulties with people. Tolerance and patience were not part of his nature; he was unable to treat fools gently or to understand that there were persons who honestly disagreed with what he believed and held dear. He enjoyed creating discomfiture, and he could be fearless before even the most august authorities if he felt his cause worthy. He inspired dismay, unquestioning loyalty, and implacable hatred, but for the most part, his ebullience, his intensity and the quantity and quality of his achievement evoked admiring and affectionate incredulity. They still do.

12

CHAPTER TWO

Prologue to Pugin's Career

January 1835 to August 1836

Pugin's preparation for life as an architect was somewhat unusual but adequate. His father, Augustus Charles Pugin (1762–1832) was an expert delineator of and authority on medieval architecture, a publisher of and dealer in books on architecture and the arts, and a notable topographical and architectural illustrator. An émigré, A.C. Pugin was enrolled as a student of the Royal Academy in March 1792; in the decade that followed, he acquired the reputation for skill, talent, precision in draughtsmanship, and for sensitivity to the elements of scenery, which were to provide him with a life-work and his family with its livelihood.

In 1802, when he was forty, A.C. Pugin married an English-woman, Catherine Welby; A. Welby Pugin, their only child, was born when his father was fifty. The establishment of a school in which young men were trained to be architectural illustrators and architects was one of the various enterprises of the senior Pugins, and their son attended and travelled with them and their students when they went to France or into the field in England to measure buildings and draw them at first hand. In the last years of the life of the elder Pugin, such expeditions were devoted to the preparation of the plates for the books he was publishing. A. W. Pugin had participated in the studies for *Examples of Gothic Architecture,* a work his father had in progress at the time of his death in 1832. Having inherited this book unfinished the younger Pugin undertook, in 1835, to complete it in order to demonstrate his skill, announce his professional aspirations, and fulfil his father's commitment to the subscribers.

Pugin's training as an architect was different from that of his contemporaries because he never served as an articled assistant

13

to a senior member of the profession. He went, instead, directly from his father's classroom into the independent pursuit of a career, first as an illustrator of medieval buildings and a designer in the decorative arts, and thence into the practice of architectural design.

Pugin's activities between January 1835 and August 1836, were the preface to his professional life. In these months he built his first building, found clients, and continued to add to his knowledge of medieval art through travel in England and on the Continent, and private research, sketching, conversations with antiquaries, as well as study in private collections.

The year 1835 began auspiciously with the purchase of a piece of land near Salisbury which, Pugin reported, commanded 'a magnificent view of the cathedral and city with the river Avon winding through the beautiful valley. . . . I have as advantageous a situation as any in England.' He was building a house for his family, which then consisted of Louisa, whom he had married in the spring of 1833, and two children, Edward Welby Pugin, born 11 March 1834, and Anne, aged two and a half, daughter of Pugin's first wife, Anne, who had died in childbirth. With boundless optimism and assurance, Pugin announced that St Marie's Grange would be 'the only modern building that is compleat in every part in the antient style'. He even planned to execute the sculpture in the chapel himself.

There were at least two designs for the house: the earlier was that illustrated in Benjamin Ferrey's biography, and the second was the one actually followed in building. Both schemes show how Pugin struggled with the problems of the site and the choice of architectural style. In spite of its beauty, the land was not ideal, for it sloped so abruptly to the river that, as he proposed to exploit the views of Longford Castle and Salisbury Cathedral, Pugin was forced to build at the upper edge of the plot and close to the road. The design shown in Ferrey's book was amateurishly French and wildly unpractical; it was a small château with a steep flight of steps on the river façade. Its plan

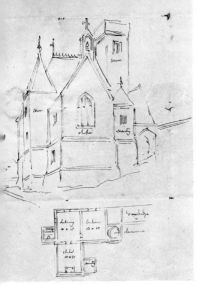

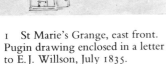

1 St Marie's Grange, east front. Pugin drawing enclosed in a letter to E. J. Willson, July 1835.

2 Photograph, St Marie's Grange, same angle as Plate 1 showing additions and changes.

was exceedingly awkward, for after climbing the stairs, one would have entered at first-floor level, turned sharply to the right, and proceeded down a long corridor, space for which was subtracted from a living room that could not afford its loss.

The final version of St Marie's Grange survives in a drawing Pugin made on the day his home was ready to receive its occupants. Unusual and distinctly personal, the house had emerged as coherent and attractive, in spite of the experimental indecision that had characterized the development of its design. The steep roofs, large tower, pyramidal sacristy roof, bell-cote, and drawbridge composed an architectural ensemble that must have startled the passengers on the coaches passing along the road.

The L-shaped house was brick with stone trim, the northeast side was composed of the high square tower, the side of the sacristy, and the windowless wall of the chapel. On the west the elevation was utilitarian: the four windows to the living rooms and the bedrooms were set in pairs with a buttress

between them. On the front facing the river, there were two windows to the left of a big chimney, the tall tower which contained the waterclosets, and the wall of the chapel. The fourth side was that in Pugin's drawing.

St Marie's Grange was small and had no hall, no staircase (save the spiral stair in the tower), and no corridors. The interior must have been snug and comfortable, with elegant details. Pugin's books were installed in shelves set into the thick walls, and the ceilings were enriched with painted inscriptions. Hull of Wardour Street had made the sturdy but attractive green leather furniture especially for the house from Pugin's own designs. The fireplaces were well proportioned and simple. Mrs Pugin's initials appeared in the spandrels of the door between the library and the chapel.

St Marie's Grange, a 'compleat building of the 15th century', was not long to be part of the Pugin story. Six months after it was finished, Pugin reported that 'Mrs Pugin does not have good health here which I suppose is owing to her removal from the sea air.' This indisposition, which was to affect the history of St Marie's Grange, seems however to have been due to

3 St Marie's Grange. The door between the library and the chapel, from a watercolour by Pugin, probable date 1835–6.

4 St Marie's Grange from the south. The bays are additions and other changes can be seen in the brickwork.

another cause, for a third child was born on 13 October 1836, when the family had been in residence a little over a year. The new house was too small almost as soon as it was completed, and in the autumn of 1837 the family left Salisbury. The house stood empty until 1840 when, realizing he would never return, Pugin decided to sell it, only to find that its peculiarities made it difficult to market.

1, 2 Sometime before 1876 major changes were made in St Marie's Grange. The ground floor on the river side was turned into a pair of living rooms and the service quarters were restricted to the north and west portions of that floor. The first floor was given over to bedrooms, one of which was made out of the chapel. The largest single change was introduced to correct the greatest inconvenience of the house – for it had suffered from the lack of an entrance hall, staircase, and corridors. Quite efficiently, by closing the L in a style in keeping with the rest of the house, all three were added. Other changes followed, although it is uncertain whether they were made when the new quarter, which made the house square, was built. The tower on the river side was tile-hung, and one gathers from Pugin's drawing that its roof may well have been changed. Bay windows were added to what was once the chapel and to the room beneath it, and a large bay was built projecting from the southwest corner of the ground floor. The chapel window disappeared in the addition of the bay on the east. The conformation of the main roof does not now match that in Pugin's sketch.

The way in which the staircase corner and many of the emendations blend with the original character of St Marie's Grange suggests that Pugin himself may have designed them. He visited Salisbury for three days in April 1841, when he could have been arranging the additions. Two months later, on the day of the consecration of St Chad's, Birmingham, he received word that the house had been sold.

It is difficult to know just how much influence St Marie's Grange had upon domestic architecture that came after it.

18

Pugin's house must have been known, for as his reputation grew, anything he designed acquired something of his notability.

Before 1836 and the building of St Marie's Grange, the larger Gothic revival houses had been either castles or Tudor-Elizabethan mansions. Smaller houses with stylistic pretensions to Gothic had alluded to, rather than reproduced, the style. They were embellished with details copied from more elaborate medieval buildings, but little beyond their ornament suggested Gothic. A vaguely ecclesiastical air was the result of the pointed windows and mouldings. Such houses were often desired as picturesque additions to landscape; their titular style had little to do with their task as functioning architecture.

Pugin's house was quite different. Idiosyncratic and hardly usable at first, it was not simply strange – for it was neither a 'Gothick' cottage nor a diminutive castle – but something new. St Marie's Grange was a reasonable reproduction of a 'compleat building of the 15th century'; it was small, severe, and homely, but it had presence. Its building materials were used, as Pugin would have said, without 'sham'; it made its statement because, from the plan to the last detail, everything harmonized with everything else and no details were applied to make the house appear to be something it was not. Scarcely a feature could be identified with those common in the earlier Gothic revival, and the whole had an unmistakable authenticity. When he resorted for his inspiration to the anonymous, vernacular house style of the English fifteenth and sixteenth centuries, Pugin introduced a kind of domestic manner hitherto unused in the nineteenth century. He also raised fundamental questions about the relationship between Gothic architecture and its superficial ornament and the proper nature of its revival.

Pugin seems to have found it reassuring to be rushed and overworked, and his hectic professional life had already begun when he moved his family from Ramsgate to Salisbury in 1835. Despite his report that he was 'overpowered by a continual succession of businesses' and in 'the thick of Catholic controversy', Pugin resolved to answer A. W. Hakewill's pamphlet

Thoughts upon the Style of Architecture to be Adopted in Rebuilding the Houses of Parliament, which had condemned Parliament's decision to require either Gothic or Elizabethan. Hakewill, who was four years older than Pugin, had set himself up as a champion of the Classical styles. He compared Gothic to a weed and Classic to a flower, a formulation which even dispassionate critics found lacking in 'good taste'. He also stated that Gothic was 'a style of doubtful origin, mute to our sympathies' and lacking in 'ease and purity of sentiment'.

Virtually everything Hakewill said might have been designed to inflame Pugin, whose short and well-phrased response, written in one day, had the tone of mature conviction, and contained the ideas on Gothic which he was later to develop. Pugin announced that if medieval architecture were 'brought in fair comparison with any other style, it must, in the mind of every impartial judge, shine with complete superiority – the grandeur of their masses – the exquisite finish of their details – their bold and scientific construction – the light, and at the same time solid, manner in which they are erected – all must fill the mind of the beholder with admiration, and a profound veneration for the skill and perseverance of the ages in which they were produced'.

'The continual succession of businesses' which Pugin had mentioned included work on two books and a number of jobs as a free-lance designer. He was preparing the plates for the four volumes of his illustrations which Ackermann was publishing; *Gothic Furniture in the style of the 15th Century* appeared in 1835, and *Designs for Iron and Brass work, Designs for gold and silversmiths, Details of ancient timber houses of the 15th and 16th Centuries* came out in 1836. At the same time he was trying to finish *Examples,* in spite of the endless complications occasioned by E. J. Willson's failure to complete the text; Willson had been the elder Pugin's collaborator, and the relationship had been inherited with the responsibility to publish the book. James Gillespie Graham and Charles Barry, two senior architects, were responsible for the demand for 'drawings and designs to be done coming from all quarters' which Pugin said he 'got through by keeping them going on together and leaving nothing quite neglected'. In the spring of 1835 Pugin designed a church for Gillespie Graham. Charles Barry had hired him to work on certain of the decorative details for the King Edward VI Grammar School in Birmingham.

Of the two accounts, Barry's was the larger and the one now more easily traced. Ten drawings entirely in Pugin's hand and twenty-seven tracings from others of his drawings are now in the collections of the Royal Institute of British Architects. They bear witness to the extent, character, and date of his contribution.

In his design for the school, Barry united an arrangement of masses and late Gothic detail in the way which, after years of work and infinite patience, care, and precision, he was to bring to maturity in the Houses of Parliament. The school also demonstrated his ability to create buildings which were both polished tributes to a historical style and useful responses to a nineteenth-century need. It is important here because the productive collaboration between Pugin and Barry was begun on this project. The ultimate responsibility for the building was in Barry's competent hands, and Pugin could work without stress or anxiety about absolute fidelity to the accuracy of Gothic stylistic details. This relationship was to be continued in the years of joint work on the Houses of Parliament.

When he hired Pugin, Barry had the design for the Birmingham school well in hand. He had been working on it since 1833, and the dates on his drawings show it was virtually finished by January 1835. In April he needed details, bosses, pendants, ceiling decorations, spandrels, brattishing, and furniture – the very things Pugin could do best. That Barry signed some of the Pugin drawings is of no consequence, for it was he who had commissioned the work and accepted responsibility for it.

The old Houses of Parliament had been in large part destroyed by fire in October 1834. When Parliament had recovered from the shock, it resolved on a competition to obtain a design for a new building and, because Westminster Hall was to be incorporated into the new complex and the site lay adjacent to Westminster Abbey, to require that the new Houses should be either Gothic or Elizabethan. From the moment these terms were announced, the competition elicited a fascinating outpouring of ideas on architectural styles, on the nature of the practice of architecture and on the procedures usual in the management of competitions. Hakewill's pamphlet and Pugin's response were part of this literature.

Barry entered the competition, and Pugin worked for him from August 1835 until the submission of designs at the end of the year. Barry won. There can be no doubt that Pugin had a hand in Barry's entry; the fact that he probably drew all of the ornamental detail and possibly all or some of the sheets submitted by Barry does not mean that Pugin was the architect of the award-winning proposal. Barry had learned how to remain the master in a working relationship with Pugin, no easy task. Pugin seems also to have prepared James Gillespie Graham's entry which did not receive a premium although it was much admired for its draughtsmanship, which was recognized to have been by the same hand as some of Barry's submissions.

It was in this way that Pugin began the largest and best known of his professional undertakings; at the same time an architectural mystery was born. After his death, and again after the death of Charles Barry, the question of the authorship of the Houses was brought to public attention in an atmosphere so unpleasant that one would wish the question not to be reopened. But it must be if Pugin is to be understood. Of the events of 1835 only one fact is certain: Pugin spent over half his time in Barry's employ between September 1835 and January 1836. That he performed the larger part of that service on the Barry competition entry seems obvious. The surviving drawings offer no solution, for only one of the many hundreds made for the Houses dates from 1835; it is in Barry's hand, but it was not one of the sheets submitted in the competition.

The year 1835 had been one of religious decision and professional promise for Pugin, but there were intimations that all was not well. His wife was frail and often ill, and Pugin had experienced an attack of the debilitating and frightening disease of the eyes, probably iritis, which was to haunt him for the rest of his life and to contribute to his collapse and death. In November, in the midst of the preparation of the competition design, he had become blind, a condition which lasted only a few days but threatened to recur. In addition, his assertiveness about his Catholicism had made life in Salisbury somewhat uneasy. A comment written at the end of 1835 conveys the mood in which Pugin greeted the year 1836. He was still optimistic, and he derived a kind of pleasure from his encounters with those who opposed him.

I have to sustain a heavy attack continually on the score of religion in which, however I consider I always come off victorious. I have since being settled in Salisbury officiated as an acolyte having no youth in our congregation capable of serving with becoming decorum. Our dresses which are handsome and quite correct were worked by the ladies of the chapel and I assure you you would hardly know me when issuing from the sacristy door in full canonicals.

5 Preliminary study for the title-page of *Contrasts*, the genesis of the plate ultimately dedicated to 'The Trade'. Pencil drawing by Pugin, 1836.

CHAPTER THREE

First Years of Practice and the Early Churches

August 1836 to August 1839

Pugin's career was to consist of three phases. The first of these began in 1836, when he became a public figure upon the publication of the first edition of *Contrasts*; it ended with the preparation of the drawings for St Chad's Cathedral, Birmingham, and those for St Michael the Archangel, Gorey, Ireland, in the spring and summer of 1839. In these years Pugin began to sense the pleasures of success, realized that his intense study of medieval art had begun to bear fruit, and acquired the clients whose support could turn his ambitions into reality. His enthusiasm for the role in which he had cast himself was boundless, and the buildings he produced between 1836 and 1839 are original, dramatic, unrestrained. They were also stylistically varied, for he had not settled into a pattern; they reveal tastes he was later to discipline or suppress.

Pugin had begun, in 1835, to assemble the ideas for the first edition of *Contrasts,* a book which was to bring him fame and enemies and establish the tone of his relationship with the architectural community. Unable to find a publisher who was willing to undertake anything so controversial, he resolved to publish the book himself. The plates were prepared with the assistance of Talbot Bury, a close friend who also had been a student at A.C. Pugin's school. The plan to argue his points largely in etchings in which nineteenth-century buildings were compared with those of the Middle Ages certainly dated to the year 1832, when Pugin had toyed with the idea of exposition through contrasted monuments. Benjamin Ferrey suggests in his biography that the method had occurred to Pugin even earlier.

Work on the sixteen plates for *Contrasts* preceded the writing of the text; the latter seems to have been secondary to the trenchant message of the illustrations. The drawings of contrasted buildings required almost no revision before they were etched; Pugin did reconsider and reorganize those for the 5 decorative title-page, 'The Balance' (which appeared finally as the tail-piece) and for the plate dedicated to architecture, 'The Trade'. Only then was he able to separate to his satisfaction the several images he had evolved.

Pugin was a brilliant satirist. At a time when many architectural journalists could turn a neat phrase and write amusingly, he emerged as conspicuously able. His acumen was matched by his unwillingness to temporize. His boldness was costly, for had he not chosen to challenge the prevailing taste and its arbiters his talent could have put him at the top of his profession. Belief in an alternative to the system it attacks is an ingredient of effective satire: Pugin was a believer.

The text of the first edition of *Contrasts* seems weak only because of the strength and assertiveness of the plates. The argument moves inexorably along its course, and the reader can resist its reasoning only if he refuses to accept any one of its premises. Pugin asserted that architecture had fallen from excellence, which he defined in the Vitruvian sense as fitness to and expression of purpose. From this safe ground he could then say that religious feeling had always evoked the finest in architectural statement. Christianity and Gothic were one, and the styles expressive of paganism were unsuitable for Christian →purposes. With the Reformation, 'the spell was broken, the Architecture itself fell with the religion to which it owed its birth'. From this point, he could set out to show how greed had moved the reformers to destroy not only the architecture and treasures of the medieval past but also the institutions which had maintained culture and a sense of man's responsibility to man. The rest of the text was Pugin's vivid and often despairing view of the architecture of his own age. His choice of verbs was devastating: the 'neat and modern churchman . . . trips from the door to the vestry' and 'goes through his prayers'; 'a solitary residentiary' may be seen 'peeping above his cushion'.

Words such as 'baneful' and 'execrable' abound; the latter was a favourite with Pugin. He thought 'the present system of church and chapel building . . . trafficking in sacred things'. Fashion had replaced art, and architecture had become a trade – a proposition he illustrated with acerbity in his first and most effective plate.

Whatever *Contrasts* cost Pugin was money well spent. The reviews ranged from angry to amused and admiring. The Salisbury papers embarked upon a campaign against him and his book which, to his vast entertainment, so encouraged its sale that only one copy of the edition remained.

As he had no pressing fresh responsibilities and the tumult over *Contrasts* was beginning to subside, Pugin went back to work for Charles Barry in the autumn of 1836 and spent what remained of the year on the further revisions of the Houses of Parliament designs. Again, the precise nature of his work for Barry is not clear. The drawings of the building, which are dated 1836, show that after this round in the campaign, in which Barry was surely the leading participant, the new Houses began to assume the appearance we know today. Several hands may be detected in the drawings; one is certainly Pugin's.

Prospects for the future were bright, for much to his delight, Pugin had received an admiring letter from the Reverend Daniel Rock, chaplain to the Earl of Shrewsbury and an antiquary of note. The illustrations in *Designs for Gold and Silversmiths* and the news of Pugin's conversion had encouraged Dr Rock to approach a young man whom he did not know. A copy of *Contrasts* was sent off to Alton Towers, and by October, Pugin was in touch with John Talbot, sixteenth Earl of Shrewsbury and Waterford. Benjamin Ferrey dates this first significant meeting in 1832, and sets it in Hull's furniture shop. Talbot Bury, who knew Pugin well and wrote his obituary in *The Builder*, left the date indefinite, while implying that it belongs in the chronology somewhere in the years 1835–6, which is doubtless correct. For all his precocity, Pugin would have had little to offer the Earl in 1832, for he had not yet become a

6 South front of Scarisbrick Hall. Pencil drawing by Pugin, *c.* 1837. The house which antedated Pugin's work at Scarisbrick is the left wing.

Catholic, resolved to become an architect, or begun his independent career.

Pugin's first major architectural commission was for Charles Scarisbrick, a Catholic bachelor of thirty-five, who had, on the death of his brother in 1833, inherited Scarisbrick Hall in Lancashire as well as great wealth. The fact that the earliest drawings Pugin prepared for him were for minor additions – a fireplace and a garden pavilion – suggests that Mr Scarisbrick had been referred to him by another architect too busy to undertake small commissions. Pugin's involvement with Scarisbrick Hall is well-documented. Volumes of drawings for the house are now in the collections of the Royal Institute of British Architects, and every sheet Pugin prepared seems to have been reverently preserved.

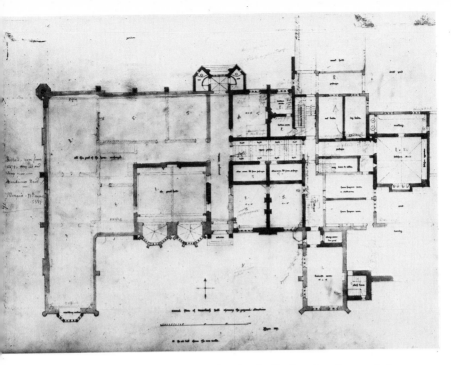

7 Scarisbrick Hall. Pencil, ink and wash drawing by Pugin, 1837. A ground plan showing the internal corridor and the proposed additions.

Scarisbrick was determined to add to and renovate but not replace old Scarisbrick Hall, which had already been considerably altered earlier in the century. In April 1837, Pugin began to prepare a portfolio setting forth his proposals for changes to the old house and his recommendations for an addition. Though he was to go on working at Scarisbrick until 1845, the programme for the house was in all its essentials laid down in 1837. This was to be the largest single domestic commission of Pugin's career and also the one most typical of his early years and youthful taste.

A quick review of the drawings Pugin made on a journey to France and the Low Countries in 1837 shows his preoccupation with the Tombeau d'Amboise and the organ case at Evreux, and with the Renaissance urn terminals of the carved fittings in the church of St Pierre, Caen; details from them were to

8   Fireplace design for the south room, old wing, Scarisbrick Hall. Ink drawing by
Pugin, *c.* 1837.

appear at Scarisbrick. On a journey in 1832 Pugin had already sketched various decorations from Ulm which were to prove useful when he came to devise the settings for Mr Scarisbrick's growing collection of sixteenth- and seventeenth-century carvings. In 1838 he was back in Germany to study the late Gothic details at Mayence. Despite what these sources suggest about the derivation of the Scarisbrick decorations, the great fireplaces, the carving about the doors, the extravagance (or is it outrageousness?) of the west rooms resemble most the frontispiece of *Contrasts* and the plates in *Details of Antient Timber Houses of the 15th and 16th Centuries*, which appeared late in 1836 or early in 1837, and Pugin's drawings for furniture and decorations which are dated 1834–5. Little about the Scarisbrick interiors prefigures the loyalty to scholarly revivalism which Pugin was to espouse. Instead, they communicate an effervescent and contagious pleasure in the use of normally-large architectural shapes reduced and utilized as a decorative lining for a room. The interiors at Scarisbrick are masterly drawings come to life. Because Charles Scarisbrick was so rich that he could afford almost anything, and because he and his architect seem to have been agreed on the results they wanted, Scarisbrick Hall was to be one of the few commissions which allowed Pugin to realize his dreams.

The planning of Scarisbrick cannot have been easy, for it was a big house and the new half had to accommodate to the older portion, which would then constitute the western wing. The north–south dimension of the earlier house established that of the block Pugin was to extend into a U-shaped structure, the major façade of which would face the grounds to the south, as its owner desired. With the audacity of youth – for the house 6 in Salisbury had been his sole preparation for the task – Pugin set to work to distribute the space into rooms and provide east – west and north – south corridor access on the two floors of his new wing, while somehow admitting daylight into the passage on the ground floor. His solution was a triumph of inventiveness: he lighted the east – west corridor with skylights,

31

and by the simple expedient of making the first-storey corridor floor half the width of the one below, he developed along the walls passages through which light could fall unimpeded to the lower corridor.

Neither the decorative exuberance of the interior of Scarisbrick Hall nor the ingenuity of the corridor design were to appear again in Pugin's work. As he came to associate Gothic revivalism with religious and ethical belief he was to turn away from stylistic mixtures. Because of its vigour and freshness, and Pugin's straightforward solution of the problem of the corridor, this design belongs among his early achievements; it suggests the architecture of ships or the galleries above the stage in a theatre. There is no documentary proof to support Benjamin Ferrey's assertion that in the 1820s and 1830s Pugin was an adventurous and intrepid sailor, but the numerous sketches of ships which appear among his drawings bear witness to his genuine preoccupation with the sea. He had surely had ample experience of the architecture of the stage, for he had worked, perhaps intermittently, as a set designer at Covent Garden between 1830 and 1833.

6   In the south front of Scarisbrick Hall, Pugin displayed for the first time preferences which were to reappear in his later occasional work on private houses. Bay windows and oriels

9   The internal corridor at Scarisbrick Hall, a view from the lobby at the foot of the staircase. Pencil drawing by Pugin, *c.* 1837.

varied the masses of façades; large areas of carefully laid masonry were relieved only by delicate details around windows and doors; the skyline was composed of a flourish of rich chimneys and lanterns; decorations included heraldic material, rebuses, and words on parapets, around doors, and in stained glass; a tall tower of delicate proportions, quite different from that ultimately built by his son E. W. Pugin, rose in an angle of the south façade. Precedents for each element of the decorative detail could be found in the English and Continental houses of the fourteenth and fifteenth centuries which Pugin had studied. Scarisbrick was not, however, a copy of any building but rather a collection of elegances extracted from many. The character of the whole was established both by the rather unsettling contrasts which Pugin developed between the big, severe planes and the small-scale, almost dainty decoration, and by the way the decorative details and large forms, such as oriels, appeared repetitiously, distributed over the rigid blocks to which they were attached.

After his work at Scarisbrick, Pugin could have become a fashionable secular architect had he cared to do so. He had displayed his talent for creating architectural fiction; he had made a house which suggested an aristocratic background and a present affluence. Scarisbrick Hall was notable for the richness of its decoration and the evidence of a youthful and vigourous personal style. Pugin was, however, no courtier, and even as he was building Scarisbrick, he had decided to expend his abilities and energy in quite other directions.

In 1836 and 1837, as his practice and reputation grew, Pugin's regular clients continued their support. Lucrative work which flowed in from James Gillespie Graham and Charles Barry supplemented the retainer paid by Mr Scarisbrick.

Pugin rushed from place to place establishing acquaintance-ships, visiting Catholic institutions, and preparing designs for the people and institutions that were to become the mainstays of his future practice. The Earl of Shrewsbury now began to

10   Interior of the chapel, Oscott College, showing Pugin's proposed decoration. Proof of an etching by Pugin, 1837. Pugin bought the Communion rail but designed the altar.

figure dramatically in Pugin's life, for earlier and preliminary meetings between Dr Rock, the Earl, and Pugin had gone well. Both gentlemen were prepared to vouch for his abilities and to act as his sponsors in Catholic circles. Early in 1837, on his way to Scarisbrick to pay one of his regular visits to supervise the building operations there, Pugin for the first time called at Oscott College, where the Earl of Shrewsbury and Dr Rock were well known. A week later he was back at Oscott, and this time he met Bishop Walsh. Accounts of what transpired on this occasion vary, but it appears that Joseph Potter of Lichfield, who had been the architect of the new college buildings, was summarily dismissed. A few weeks later Pugin prepared an illustration of his proposal for the decoration of the chapel at

34

Oscott: the College had found a new architect. At the end of the year, Pugin was lecturing to the Oscott students, preparing drawings for the Earl of Shrewsbury, Dr Rock, and John Hardman, a Birmingham manufacturer of buttons and other metal objects. At about the same time, Ambrose Phillipps entertained Pugin at Grace Dieu House in Leicestershire. In December Pugin met the Right Reverend Dr Thomas Griffiths, Bishop of the London District, to discuss the project of building a great new church in Southwark.

Reviews of *Contrasts* were appearing in 1837; Pugin could bask in the praises – a few enthusiastic, many amused, and others grudging – which the book brought him. He may not have been loved in some quarters, but he was certainly noticed. The number of orders he had begun to receive for metalwork and ecclesiastical fittings, such as altars, showed that his abilities as an artist and his ideas of the taste that should prevail were beginning to be accepted: his career was launched.

What with work in Lancashire, new-found friendships in the Midlands, and a study journey to the Low Countries and northern France, Pugin was in Salisbury only a third of the days of the first six months of 1837. In September Mrs Pugin came up to London, and the family took lodgings in Chelsea.

One can well believe Pugin's postscript to a letter written on 27 August 1837: 'Could you but see me at Oscott you would hardly credit me to be the same individual that you remember *some years ago.*' Any shyness or uncertainty had evaporated in the warmth of the reception of his person, ideas, and gifts. With astonishing self-confidence, arising from his belief in a cause he thought just, and before he had ever built a church or indeed much of anything, Pugin reported jubilantly in February 1838 that he had accepted commissions for no less than ten churches in England and two in Ireland!

Such sudden success was not designed to endear him to other architects forced to sit back and watch him gather in work for which they had been waiting. Nor was Pugin gracious about the disappointment his popularity brought others. When

Edward James Willson (1787–1854) protested that he had been promised the commission for the new church in Derby, Pugin responded tartly that work was already under way, that he could not 'make difficulties' but only go on 'as fast as possible for the interests of religion demand that a new church shortly be raised'. Even though he entered practice with opinion running in his favour, he should have foreseen that his success would soon be contested.

Pugin found time to write and publish in 1838 and 1839 although he was busy, often exhausted, sometimes ill, and in many ways tried beyond the limits of his short patience. He wrote because he was 'determined to be a very sword against all protestant writers on Catholic art' and because he found solace in his wit and ability to express his anger in words. In the summer of 1838, in spite of the confusion of his many tasks and the desperation bred of his perfectionist demands on himself and everyone associated with him, he produced a classic example of Pugin prose on the subject of the portraits which graced what he called 'the annual exhibitions':

What loads of ill-painted faces line the rooms; what heaps of miniatures in round, square, black, gilt, and all sorts of frames; curly-headed boys with hoops; boarding school misses feeding kittens; tight-laced and ringleted young ladies dressed for the ball-room; school boys galloping on ponies; sprucely dressed men looking inconceivably silly; ladies playing with poodles and fans, or vacantly staring; portly citizens and old beaux – all are to be found to the life; then the family group, with the mamma reclining carelessly on a sofa in the centre, the pet at her side, the elder daughters copying flowers and tambour working, the husband surveying the whole group with great complacency, while the fore-ground is filled up by the more juvenile branches stuffing fruit or breaking toys, and the portly form of a nurse entering in the background with a jumping squaller completes the tableau.

Such frivolities were perfectly suited for non-Catholics, said Pugin, but he urged his co-religionists to be painted with crucifixes and rosaries rather than with decanters and flower pots, and went on to warn them that: 'The truth is the air we breathe is so infected with the pestilence of Protestantism that it either withers or stints every Catholic blossom.' ⟵

The hyperbole, the intense feeling, and the wit of his descriptions go far to explain Pugin's rapid rise to prominence. Out of his puritanism, he poured forth reasons for the secession of English Catholics from a cosy and materialistic nineteenth-century society, which he made to look not only ridiculous but dissolute. Pugin's admiration for Savonarola should come as no surprise. Something of the same quality that distinguished his writing was to appear in even his earliest churches; they ⟵ possessed the same assurance of righteousness, drama of succinctness, excitement and freshness of expression. He put his acute powers of observation and memory, his taste and artistic discrimination at the service of his religious conviction and will to reform: he sought to instruct English Catholics in the history and traditions of their faith and to revive the art associated with the practice of that faith.

The ten churches to which Pugin referred in February 1838, were St Mary's, Derby; St James', Reading; St Mary's, Uttoxeter; St Augustine's, Solihull; Our Lady and St Thomas *11, 12* of Canterbury, Dudley; St Marie's, Southport; St Ann's, Keighley; a church now replaced by the present St Hilda's, Whitby; St George's, Southwark; and a church in Manchester which never materialized. To these should be added the following projects on which he was also working: the decorations for the chapel at Oscott College, and the chapel building *10* of St Peter's College, Wexford. He may also have designed the *13* little village church at Bree, near Enniscorthy, the plans for *14* which, in an Irish version of the story, were obtained from Pugin by J. H. Talbot of Waterford. The strange church at Ramsgrange near Wexford may also belong to these years, but if he had anything to do with its design, Pugin certainly did not supervise its construction.

11　St Augustine's Solihull, an early and primitive Pugin parish church.

12　Our Lady and St Thomas of Canterbury, Dudley, built for the Hon. and Reverend George Spencer at a cost of £3165, which included its decoration.

13　The chapel, St Peter's College, Wexford.

14　The parish church, Bree, Wexford.

Of all these early buildings, the churches at Reading and Derby are the best known and most often discussed. The drawings for several had been prepared and construction had begun before George Myers, the competent builder who was to share many of Pugin's responsibilities, appeared on the scene. In his obituary of Pugin, Talbot Bury said that St Mary's, Derby, was the first church on which the two men had collaborated. Since there is positive evidence that Myers prepared the estimates for St Wilfrid's, Hulme, in October 1838, the foundation of his close association with Pugin may certainly be dated in that year.

St James', Reading, the first church Pugin designed, was to be a disappointment to its architect. Begun in the last weeks of 1837, it was not opened until 1840, months after his other churches coeval with it had been completed. The untimely death of James Wheble, its benefactor, occasioned the delay.

St James' was in the Norman style because it was to stand adjacent to the ruins of an abbey. Norman was not Pugin's *métier*; yet it was not the style but a variety of other reasons that caused him to disown St James' after its completion. He did not attend its opening, and he did not include it among his accomplishments in the frontispiece of *An Apology for the Revival of Christian Architecture in England* (1843) where he illustrated the buildings of which he was proud.

Pugin seems not to have abandoned St James' before it was finished, but ever afterward, when it was mentioned, he announced that out of justice to himself he wished it known that difficulties had developed there which led to false economies and artistic disasters which were not his responsibility. At Reading Pugin encountered forceful resistance to his ideas for the first time. He had designed the presbytery in the manner of the Jew's House at Lincoln, carefully arranging it so that neither it nor the church would trespass upon the ruins of the abbey, but his plans were set aside and part of the house which was constructed lay within the abbey foundations. He had

15

15 Pugin illustrated the churches of which he was proud for his frontispiece drawing to *An Apology for the Revival of Christian Architecture*, giving to many spires they were never to acquire.

In this plate, and occasionally in his writing, Pugin employed the archaic spelling of *Marie* for *Mary*. At other times, for example, in his discussion of his churches in *The Present State of Ecclesiastical Architecture in England*, he used *Mary* instead of *Marie*. In all cases the dedication is properly *Mary*.

1. St George's Southwark, London
2. St Peter's, Woolwich
3. St Marie's, Stockton-on-Tees
4. St Giles', Cheadle
5. St Marie's, Newcastle-on-Tyne
6. North Gate, St Marie's, Oscott
7. St Austin's, Kenilworth
8. Jesus Chapel, Pontefract
9. Cathedral, Killarney
10. St Chad's, Birmingham
11. St Oswald's, Liverpool
12. Holy Cross, Kirkham
13. St Barnabas', Nottingham
14. Gorey, Ireland
15. St Marie's, Derby
16. St Alban's, Macclesfield
17. St Marie's, Brewood
18. St Winifride's, Shepshead
19. St Andrew's, Cambridge
20. St Bernard's Priory, Leicestershire
21. St Marie's, Keighley
22. St Marie's, Warwick Bridge
23. St Wilfrid's, Manchester
24. St Marie's, Southport

prepared a scheme of painted decorations for the apse in which details taken from manuscript illuminations were combined in a manner inspired by the medieval wall-painting he had studied in Barfreston church in Kent; this, too, had been discarded in favour of a meagre display of unsuitable and ugly foliage.

In August 1839, the Earl of Shrewsbury attended the opening ceremonies at St Mary's, Uttoxeter, the first of Pugin's churches to be completed. The Honourable and Reverend George Spencer, an 1832 convert and priest at West Bromwich, led the service and the assembled company included the Prince and Princess Doria Pamphili, son-in-law and daughter of the Earl, and J. H. Talbot of Waterford. St Mary's had been built entirely at the Earl's expense.

Had Pugin not written a description of St Mary's when he finished it his religious and artistic intentions would now be difficult to understand, for the church has been extensively modified. The chancel has been rebuilt, aisles have been added to Pugin's nave, and a porch has been placed across the front.

After announcing in his description that this church was 'the first Catholic structure erected in this country in strict accordance with the rules of ancient ecclesiastical architecture since the days of the pretended reformation', Pugin scarcely mentioned the exterior and never explained that the church had no aisles. He launched instead into a detailed account of the interior appointments, their significance in ancient practice and their history. After a single passing reference to the dark, stained roof, he turned to the three windows in the east and to the altar with its triptych reredos, enriched with eight angels in niches and arranged so that it could be closed during Lent. Three lamps hung before the altar, and Pugin planned that the Blessed Sacrament should be suspended over it in the form of a silver dove. Damask curtains on cranes sheltered the altar from draughts. To the right in the sanctuary were sacrarium and sedilia, and in the left wall there was an arch and tomb for the reservation of the Blessed Sacrament on Maundy Thursday. A delicate arched rood separated the chancel from the nave. After he built and equipped St Mary's, the chancels of all Pugin's churches contained at least these liturgical fundamentals. There was no screen; Pugin's battle for screens was yet to come.

Although Pugin's published statement emphasized the sanctuary and its decoration rather than the design of the building as a whole, he had in fact worked out at Uttoxeter a pattern for his small parish churches which those at Keighley, Solihull, Southport, Whitby, and Radford were to follow. If the church at Bree is by Pugin, it too represents this formula.

These early Pugin churches could hardly have been less ostentatious, for they consisted of a nave without aisles, a chancel carefully expressed by a roof lower than that of the nave, and a bell-cote placed either above the chancel arch or over the main door. St Mary's was brick with stone trim, but Pugin preferred stone if he could get it. The big, circular window over the door at St Mary's pleased him, but in more straitened circumstances Pugin was forced to be content with only narrow pointed windows. Buttresses were not a necessity; the church at Solihull, for example, had none. Modest buildings, they were shells to enclose Pugin's two minimal requirements; a nave of impressive height, and a chancel fitted in a traditional English Catholic manner, as richly as the resources of the parish would allow. They were inventions rather than revivals.

16 St Anne's, Keighley. The door is a recent addition, the sanctuary is now the entrance.

Pugin was in earnest when he said, 'I may state the present building at Uttoxeter as an instance that a Catholic church, complete in every respect, may be erected for a very moderate sum'; but he did not intend that all churches should be as limited as St Mary's, nor did he believe that St Mary's was truly Gothic. He was, rather, counselling an order of precedence in which the chancel came first. Beyond the chancel, into the nave, and on to the exterior, the statement of purpose should be made through the revival of 'the ancient ecclesiastical ← architecture of England . . . so interwoven with our holy and ancient faith . . . so appropriate for Catholic devotions . . . so associated with every recollection that should bind the Catholic of this day with the faith of his fathers'.

The simplicity of these small, early churches was to be their undoing. What had seemed adequate to a mid-nineteenth-century parish that had previously had no church soon ceased to be either large or opulent enough. When additions were made, Pugin was not there to design them and his style had gone into eclipse. The church at Keighley has been turned around, so now one enters beneath what was the chancel window, and an added aisle quite changes the interior. St Marie's, Southport, has been so rebuilt that only suggestions of Pugin's work remain. A porch has been added to St Augustine's, Solihull, and the chancel has been rebuilt. A big porch has, in the last decade, been built across the front at Dudley. St Hilda's, Whitby, has been replaced by a larger building. The church at Reading has been greatly altered and enlarged.

Begun in December 1837, and opened twenty-two months later, St Mary's, Derby, provided an opportunity for first-hand study of a major Pugin church. Many people were interested, for Pugin's sudden fame and his literary performances had begun to assume the proportions of a legend. St Mary's, his first large parish church, did its architect credit.

Because of its late Gothic style and the scholarship displayed in its details and fittings, and most of all because of its superficial resemblance to St George's, Birmingham (1820–3), St Mary's is often compared with the works of Thomas Rickman. In its richness, though not in its style, it can bear comparison with a more distinguished Rickman church, St Peter's, Hampton Lucy.

The best index to the quality of St Mary's is, however, to be found in the comments made at the time of its opening. Connoisseurs of church buildings abounded in the 1840s, and it was fashionable to be highly critical. St Mary's did not remain unchallenged in the forum of its own time, but it was generally well received. One notice said the church was a 'painfully beautiful structure' because it exposed the feeble building activities of the Church of England. In spite of limited funds and a site which offered few amenities and many problems, Pugin had convincingly revived the style of the reign of Henry VI, in a church which also displayed flashes of piquant originality.

The church lay with its axis north–south, the tall tower in the centre of the south front. The north end was composed of the chancel with a sacristy on either side of it; Edward Welby Pugin was to add the north–west chapel in 1854. Pugin had experimented with a plan in which the church crossed the site with its altar in the east, but finding it impossible to obtain enough nave with such an arrangement, he accepted a non-canonical orientation. As though to compensate for this impropriety, he designed an elaborate north extension which, for lack of money, could not be constructed when the church was built. He hoped the north chapels would one day be his to complete.

The exterior of St Mary's is unsurprising; the buttresses are thin and tall and the walls of the aisles are high and unadorned, enlivened only by the large windows. The church seems cramped in its quarters, and today, with a huge road below its south front, it also seems bleak and forlorn. The tower (which was built) and the spire (which never was) would have composed

THE NEW CATHOLIC CHURCH OF ST MARIES DERBY.

17 St Mary's, Derby, an etching by Pugin prepared at the time the church was opened. The terrace and stairs, like the spire, were never built. The presbytery (now demolished) which stood to the right of the church resembled the house shown here.

a fragile but noble street front rising two hundred feet. The flaw in the design lay in the strained relationship between the width of the church and the height of its tower and spire. Pugin seems to have seen this difficulty and in his etching to have disguised it by stressing the staircase and placing houses of the right period on either side of the front. A number of medieval motifs were woven into the design of tower and spire and the approaches to the church; the tower of Magdalen College and the setting of St Mary's, Redcliffe, occurred to Pugin's contemporaries.

At the time it was built, and since, critics have commented on the symmetry of St Mary's. In 1840 one astute and caustic observer said the church looked as though it was 'advancing in a rampant manner tower foremost' in what he called 'a flagrant demonstration of a different and modern alien origin'. It is now usual to attribute any plan with the tower in the centre of the front to the early Gothic revival. In this case, it is difficult to see what else Pugin could have done with the given site. His resolution of the difficulties suggests practicality rather than a youthful reliance on earlier patterns, though his lack of experience emerged in the disparate proportions of the parts of the building. It was to be several years before he had sufficient mastery to create a truly coherent whole.

As soon as one steps into the interior, comparison of St Mary's with earlier Gothic revival churches seems less important. Its space and decoration, although similar to other churches, is somehow different, and it is the difference that matters. The nave is eighty feet long, twenty-five feet wide, and fifty-two feet high – dramatic enough proportions in themselves; they are underscored by the splendid and eccentric arcades, thin in section and unbroken by capitals, that dominate the space. Pugin stressed these arcades in the etching of the interior he prepared when the church was opened. The etching also indicates that he never intended the interior to be painted as it now is. The bare stone, with its horizontal courses and subtle colour, would have been more airy and infinitely less mechanical and hard. The nave was lighted by the twenty clerestory windows and the windows in the aisles; its illumination must have contrasted effectively with the twilight of the chancel, coloured by its stained glass.

St Mary's was also notable because there, for the first time, Pugin was able to relate the iconography and ornament to the proportions of interior spaces and the dimensions of the architectural elements which bounded them. The angel corbels,

NEW CATHOLIC CHVRCH OF ST MARIES. DERBY.

18   Interior, St Mary's, Derby, an etching by Pugin to accompany his view of the exterior (Plate 17).

19   Interior of St Mary's as it appears today. The rood was added between the preparation of the etching (Plate 18) and the formal opening of the church.

the slender vertical mouldings of the original reredos (the one now in the church is not that in Pugin's etching) against which the horizontal of the altar came forward dramatically, and the carved pinnacles of the reredos and tabernacle seen in silhouette against the stained glass – all of these were pure Pugin.

Accounts of the church written on the occasion of its opening describe the rood, which for some reason Pugin did not include in his illustration. Rising from angel corbels, the points of its departure from the walls surmounted by standing angels holding candles, the beam arches upward as though in response to the roof of the choir and to the division between the choir and nave which it crosses. The inspiration for its design may have come from the rood on the screen of St Elizabeth's, Marburg, but, as with the arcades of the nave, Pugin's contribution lay in his feeling for the dramatic possibilities of size. The German example is much smaller.

When St Mary's was dedicated in October 1839, with a splendid procession and ceremony, it was equipped with altar candlesticks, lamps, a processional cross and candlesticks, a gilt tabernacle, altar curtains, and other metal ornaments and vessels made from Pugin designs by John Hardman of Birmingham. In the year 1838 Hardman had joined forces with Pugin to manufacture ecclesiastical metalwork and church fittings. The objects at St Mary's composed the first major collection produced by the two associates in what was to become a successful business venture.

Clergy from Oscott College officiated at the ceremony. The Reverend Francis Cheadle said the Mass, and the Very Reverend Dr Wiseman preached the sermon, for he was in England on a journey from Rome undertaken 'to promote as much as was in my powers the interest of God and his Holy Religion' – by which he meant that he had arrived to speak to the English Bishops about their resolution to detach their agent in Rome from the influence of the English College. Dr Wiseman's presence was not all that foreshadowed things that were to come. Pugin had arranged to have the vestments used at the dedication made in the revived style he preferred. The Right Reverend John Briggs, Vicar Apostolic of Yorkshire, took grave exception to Pugin's innovations, saying, 'I could have fancied myself attending a mass in the Greek church'. He wrote to the Right Reverend Peter Baines urging him to consult Propaganda about 'this irregularity'.

Pugin was not to have clear sailing in the programme of artistic reforms he proposed for the English Catholic community, but he was to have powerful allies in his cause. In March 1840, Propaganda had still not responded to Dr Baines' report, and he was vexed that 'the patrons of those vestments are crowing victory and saying that they are preferred in Rome and recommended for general adoption'.

Pugin prepared the drawings for St Alban's, Macclesfield, and for the churches in Dudley and Hulme, in October and November 1838, as St Mary's, Derby, was under construction.

The foundation stone of St Alban's was laid in April 1839, with pomp and celebration. A procession, which included churchwardens in fifteenth-century costume carrying banners and a large silver cross, marched through the streets to the site. Pugin was among the marchers, bearing the silver trowel. He must have winced at the sight and the sound of the groups at the rear of the column, which included the bands and the assembled membership of the Female Sick Club, the Sick Club of St Patrick and St Bridget, and the Hibernian Societies, all decorated with green rosettes and harps. Macclesfield received its new church with dignity, for there was 'not one yell of "No Popery", not one groan for Romanism'. The Reverend Dr Rock, in white and gold vestments, laid the stone, and the Honourable and Reverend George Spencer preached the sermon.

St Alban's continued and developed the manner of St Mary's, Derby. The nave was eighty feet long, as in St Mary's, but since the site permitted it, the church was five feet wider. The major difference between the two was the height of the nave, *20* which at St Alban's was eleven feet higher. In spite of this astonishing vertical dimension, it does not seem as tall as St Mary's because Pugin used clustered piers with capitals. The aisle windows seem smaller because they are set in large wall surfaces, and the inert wall above the chancel arch contributes to the feeling that the interior is a collection of carefully wrought parts disposed within the big space. In the months since Derby was begun, Pugin's preferences had tightened and become more strictly Perpendicular.

The screen carries a rood loft and a rood, the figures on the rood being fifteenth-century works restored by Pugin to their original colours. St Mary's, Derby, had no screen; St Alban's had the first and one of the finest rood-screen compositions Pugin was ever to produce. The churches at Dudley and Southport, of roughly the same date as St Alban's, also had screens, probably less rich and elaborate.

Pugin's wish to preserve and restore old screens and construct new ones sprang from deep personal feeling beyond mere obeisance to tradition. That he conceived his churches as growing outward from the altar is confirmed by his account of St Mary's, Uttoxeter, and by his descriptions of others of his buildings. The chancels he designed and fitted up with metalwork, tiles, stained glass, sculpture, fabrics and vestments were richly appointed chambers in which the solemn drama of the Mass could be reverently performed. A screen was essential, for without it the chancel would have seemed but an adjunct to the nave, and the profound difference of its function would have been undefined. He found innumerable medieval screens to justify his preference; indeed, his feeling for this form of enrichment grew with his scholarship. Pugin did not value the manner of worship more than the fact of it; he wanted everything to be perfect, which meant to him not only the restoration of the artistic style appropriate to his purpose, but also a return to the dignity of the medieval church and its faith. His definition of 'fitness' included the mood, the colour, and the customs and religious practices of the past.

20 The nave, St Alban's, Macclesfield. The screen and rood are by Pugin, the pulpit by E. W. Pugin and designed in 1854.

Pugin's loyalty to religious tradition and his conviction that truth in Christian art, architecture and the decorative arts required the Gothic, led him to oppose the Classical styles for such purposes. He declared that he was prepared to pursue such a policy even if he did so 'at cost of personal benefit, or of being branded with the title of fanatic'. The opening of the church of St Francis Xavier in Hereford in 1839 provided such an occasion: the building, an imitation of the Treasury of the Athenians at Delphi, together with the character of the dedication services were enough to evoke his public condemnation: 'What, then, must be the mortification to every faithful heart when it is known that, instead of being a revival of ancient glory in the opening of this new church, the dignity of religion has been shamefully degraded; the building and the service being alike lamentable – the former a modern erection, in the very worst style – the latter a morning concert, far more suited to the Hanover Rooms than the precincts of a church.' He further noted wryly that 'the *star* of the day was not the Bishop, but Madame Stockhausen', a singer whose name appeared in huge capitals on the bills advertising the occasion.

As early as 1838, in lectures to the students at Oscott, Pugin had taken a position on the artistic revival and the Church which would involve him in the struggle for screens and in altercations with most highly placed opponents.

All I have to implore you is to study the subject of ecclesiastical architecture with true Catholic feeling. Do not consider the restoration of ancient art as a mere matter of taste, but remember that it is most closely connected with the revival of the faith itself, and which all important object must ever demand our most fervent prayers, and unwearied exertions.

St Alban's, Macclesfield, was opened in 1841, only a few weeks before St Chad's, Birmingham. Everyone seemed responsive to the splendour of its appointments and stained glass, to which the Earl of Shrewsbury had contributed heavily, but there were suggestions that 'the critical eye will not fail to discover some defects which injure its external appearance'. The massive tower was not finished, and it never has been brought up to the one-hundred-foot height Pugin proposed. The tower, however, was not one of the 'defects' referred to; St Alban's suffered on the exterior as in the interior from the same disunity of part and whole. The tower dominated the front, and the transition to the aisle roofs was harsh. The church was big, but the buttresses were unduly slender. St Alban's was clumsy but remarkable, and nowhere was this clearer than at the eastern end where the ponderous chancel rose, a great, bold space, related to the nave but, because of its special function, clearly differentiated from it.

Pugin was aware that the church he had built at Dudley and opened in December 1840 was solid and effective, and he was proud of its relatively low cost. When he described it as 'small and simple', he was, in effect, saying that the building differed in character as well as in proportion from his dramatic achievements at Derby and Macclesfield.

The roof of the church at Dudley is lower in relation to width of the nave than those at either Derby or Macclesfield; hence, the Dudley church sits on the ground instead of soaring above it. Pugin was beginning to establish a delicate, if still tentative, identification between building and site. The pitch of the roofs is comfortable and wide, the angle of the nave roof being slightly more acute than that of the aisle roofs. There is a shallow clerestory of one small pointed window to each bay.

21   The west front, St Alban's, Macclesfield.

22   The east elevation, St Alban's, Macclesfield.

The exterior walls are low. The site slopes sharply to the north, and only that elevation is tall enough to require buttresses. The ashlar masonry, with narrow courses at the line of the springing of the window arches, displays a sensitivity to materials which Pugin had not demonstrated in his earlier designs; the equations established between the stone and the forms constructed of it are legible in the texture of the walls.

St Wilfrid's, Hulme, confirmed what the church in Dudley had suggested. Pugin was rapidly evolving a less ornate, freer, and more structurally expressive style. Faced with a situation at Hulme in which he was required to build a big church at small cost, Pugin chose brick and spent almost nothing on details or ornament, save in the chancel. Even there he postponed some of the embellishment until funds were available, with the result that he was still working on the decorations in 1849.

St Wilfrid's showed that Pugin had learned much in his few months of practice and that he had acquired sufficient confidence to discard his own earlier manner. The church is impressive, well composed, and in a significant way, original. Stringent economy had helped rather than hindered; as he was unable to indulge in the opulence of Derby and Macclesfield, he had been forced to concentrate on the composition of masses. It is fortunate that the spire, incorporated in the design in the frontispiece to *An Apology*, was never built, for it was an architectural extravagance which would have contradicted the pervasive simplicity of the exterior.

15

Even in its present condition – for St Wilfrid's has lost its original setting and its tower – the church is remarkable, not because it is startling but rather because it now seems commonplace. The exterior is unpretentious. The pitch of the roofs, the adequate but undramatic buttresses which join the ground courses at the stone weatherings, the English bond of the walls, and the precise stonework of the details express an intelligent appreciation of the principles of medieval building. St Wilfrid's

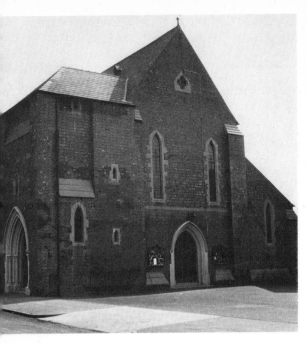

23　The west front and north aisle, St Wilfrid's, Hulme. The windows in the aisle roofs are recent additions.

24　The nave roof, St Wilfrid's.

25　The nave, St Wilfrid's. The interior is now painted. Pugin altar.

was also the first church in which Pugin placed the tower at the end of an aisle rather than on the west front – an indication of a break with his earlier formula of rigid rectangular symmetry.

25 The interior was as modest as the exterior. There were no tall columns, no startling proportions. The chancel, which had all the required features, was designed to be richly appointed. Because the windows were small the church was dark, but the contrast between the brilliant light of the eastern chamber and 24 the dimness of the nave, with its delicate but beautiful wooden roof, must have been effective.

Pugin seems to have understood that St Wilfrid's was one of his finest buildings, despite its lack of ornateness. Within the means at his disposal, he had fulfilled every religious and aesthetic requirement he had laid down. In the struggle with circumstances, he had made a statement based on principles.

Pugin sailed into 1839 assured of the support of the Earl of Shrewsbury, who, in addition to generous contributions to the building of churches, had given him the responsibility for the continued development of Alton Towers, his great country mansion in Staffordshire. The churches at Derby and Macclesfield were rising, and commissions for a dozen smaller ones, some of which were already under construction, had come his way. He was lecturing at Oscott College, where he saw himself as a missionary for Catholic art and its history. He had been welcomed in Ireland, where he was building the chapel at St Peter's College in Wexford; an Irish journalist had described him as 'a restorer of the ancient ecclesiastical architecture . . . as able with his pen classically and learnedly to unfold and defend, as he is with his pencil accurately to delineate'. His practice had become more varied, for he was working not only on churches and houses but also on the designs for the convent in Bermondsey, the first of the many conventual projects which he executed in the course of his career. Scarisbrick Hall, too, was progressing.

Pugin acted from a position of strength in first refusing to be

26 Pugin's ink and wash drawing of his rejected proposal of 1839 for St George's, Southwark. The offices and presbytery were built essentially as shown.

associated with the plans for a new church in Southwark when the committee made what he considered captious objections to his design. So began the haggling which was to bedevil the building history of St George's. Pugin was called back, a compromise was reached, and he accepted the commission, only to meet endless and distressing difficulties until the day the cathedral was opened in 1848.

The drawings Pugin prepared for Mr Byrne (the Dublin architect, who had primary charge of the design for the Loreto Abbey church at Rathfarnham), those for the church of St Michael the Archangel, Gorey, the ill-fated proposal for St George's, and the drawings for St Chad's Cathedral, Birmingham – all were done between March and June 1839. They marked the end of the first phase of Pugin's career. The diversity that, until 1840, he was willing to entertain, was

28, 29, 30

27   Interior view of the proposal for St George's, 1839. (See Plate 26.)

28   A study for the chapel, Loreto Abbey, Rathfarnham, or a design actually submitted. Pencil drawing by Pugin, 1839.

29   Proposed design for the sanctuary, chapel, Loreto Abbey, Rathfarnham. Pencil drawing by Pugin, 1839.

30   The chapel, Loreto Abbey, Rathfarnham. 1839.

expressed in the Norman of Gorey, the German Gothic of St Chad's, the late English Gothic of the first St George's scheme, and the resemblance of the Rathfarnham design to the lantern of Ely. For the moment, he had set aside the possibility raised at St Wilfrid's.

St Chad's was Pugin's first large church intended for use as a cathedral, and he met the challenge it presented without trepidation. The contract drawings were prepared in March 1839. Everything about the project seemed promising: George Myers was to be his builder; the clients included men whom Pugin trusted and liked; Birmingham, a centre of Catholic affairs, was already establishing artistic standards for other less enlightened Districts, and its historical associations with the Right Reverend Dr John Milner, whose books Pugin admired, made the building of an impressive church there an inspiring prospect. From the laying of the foundation stone in October 1839, to the ceremony of dedication on 21 June 1841, Pugin fought for his design. He despaired over each curtailment in his plans, and his spirits rose with each victory over opposition.

Shortly after the contract drawings were signed, Pugin wrote to E.J. Willson about St Chad's. He said little about the details of the building he proposed; his enthusiasm was directed elsewhere.

Of course you have heard of the great church I have begun at Birmingham. I think you will be much pleased with it. It is on a vast scale, 60 feet wide, 80 high, 168 long, with chapels, crypt etc. The style corresponds to about our Henry the 3rd or Edward the 1st and though very plain outside it will introduce a glorious internal effect, purple with stained glass and rich with gilding with everything, even vestments in character.

The descriptions of St Chad's which were published when it was opened were based on a statement Pugin issued to the representatives of the press. Since the newspaper reports resemble one another and all have the stamp of his style, one can assume that they fairly represent his thought and decisions.

The new church, Pugin said, was to be very 'plain' because 'funds being inadequate for the general employment of stone . . . it was considered more suitable to the dignity of religion to curtail external ornament, and expend the principal part of the resources in the internal construction, so as to render the place where the faithful assemble, and where the holy sacrifice is offered up, somewhat suitable to its sacred destination'. Reading between these lines one can conclude that when he learned the church had to be brick Pugin went searching for examples to follow and found them in Germany. The report continued: 'The exterior of St Chad's, like the cathedral at Munich, presents little more than a mass of perforated brick walls and high roofs', but, it went on, the interior was splendid with 'solid masonry'. The summary of the reasoning behind all of this was surely quoted directly from Pugin: 'It must be readily admitted that to have sacrificed the internal splendour of the house of God for the sake of exterior display, would have been utterly departing from true Catholic principles.'

31   St Chad's Cathedral, Birmingham. The baptistry at the left is a later addition.

In spite of the fact that only one of the spires of St Chad's had been built when the cathedral was opened – the second was not completed until after Pugin's death – the west front gave its architect satisfaction. The stained glass windows were installed; the portal in the style of 'many continental churches' was complete with its figure of the Virgin under a canopy between a pair of incensing angels, a motif which was to appear in innumerable Pugin decorations; the doors with their huge hinges resembled 'the western doors of Lichfield . . . and those of the Chapter House of York'. Pugin added in his description that, 'the caps, corbels, foliage, and other details have been faithfully reproduced from original authorities, and may be considered as the most successful revivals of ancient ornaments that have yet been achieved.'

The interior of St Chad's was splendid; it still is, although it has lost its handsome screen and the other fittings it originally possessed. The narrow and constricting site required a church that went up rather than out, a restriction that perfectly suited

32 The nave, St Chad's Cathedral, Birmingham. The screen has been removed and the interior redecorated, much of the painting being a renewal of the original.

33 The roof at the crossing, St Chad's Cathedral.

Pugin's preferences. Every part of the interior he designed participates in the beautifully exploited verticality and slenderness. Massiveness is no part of the language of the building. The twelve clustered piers are set closer together than those of St Alban's, Macclesfield, and they rise through the space to the arches beneath a wooden roof so delicate that, with the

33 brilliant diapering between the rafters, it resembles fabric stretched over a lattice. In St Chad's it is seventy-five feet from the ridge of the roof to the pavement of the nave, a measurement more than twice that of the width of the nave. The aisles are almost as high as the nave (the one on the gospel side is wider than the other).

Because Pugin was unalterably opposed to galleries in churches, that in the west end of St Chad's has occasioned comment. Pugin appears to have considered that he had not built a true gallery, but rather 'a loft for choristers', which he described as being surrounded by an 'open screen', of which no trace remains today. St Chad's was famous for its choir, in which John Hardman, who gave the cathedral its fine organ, was much interested. Had there been a true gallery in 1841, Pugin's critics would surely have mentioned it at the time, but no reference to it was made in the various reviews of St Chad's.

The interior fittings were Pugin's main concern; in the description of this, as of his other churches, three-quarters of his discussion of St Chad's was devoted to the furniture, its symbolism, and the history of the medieval objects which the Earl of Shrewsbury purchased and presented to the cathedral. The screen was a little gallery in itself. Pugin explained that all but two of the bosses in the string course of the loft were fifteenth-century carvings, the figures on the rood were ancient; and that on each bay of the screen there were thirteenth-century figures of prophets. The carved pulpit came from a church in Belgium; to it, Pugin had fitted a sounding board, stairs, and a canopy of his own design. The rich stalls were German fourteenth-century, and the figure of Our Lady on the pillar between the choir and St Marie's Chapel was a fifteenth-century original. Old triptychs hung along the walls of the aisles, and one graced the Lady Chapel. The glory of the collection of ecclesiastical antiquities was the great lectorium, which has now found its way to the Metropolitan Museum in New York. As though he were running to keep up with the quantity and quality of these 'real things', Pugin added that he had designed the sedilia after those in Westminster Abbey.

Because the site sloped abruptly and the nave floor was two feet above ground level on the west and forty feet above it on the east, Pugin decided to create a crypt in the space beneath the east end. Under the altar he placed a chapel entered through a Norman arch; running west from it a corridor twelve feet wide led 'to arched chapels on either side, each the width of a compartment of the upper church'. Pugin hoped that these would become family chantries. No 'Pagan emblems such as urns, torches, wreaths etc. nor Protestant and pompous inscriptions' were to be allowed in this undercroft.

By the time St Chad's was dedicated, the glass of the choir windows – which had been made by Warrington – was already installed. Pugin had waited for the moment when he would see his design emerge 'purple with stained glass and rich with gilding'. The painted decoration of the interior – for Pugin planned so to enrich 'the spandrels, arches and walls', as well as the roof – was still not completed. The decoration of the undercroft in 'the true style of Christian art' was also yet to come. Enough was ready, however, to give the architect ample reason for pride, although he was quoted as saying that at St Chad's, as elsewhere, 'the defects may be considered as his own, while the beauties and merits must in justice be attributed to the glorious race of old Catholic artists, whose noble works he is so zealously striving to restore'.

Today the brick neighbourhood in which St Chad's once stood like a tall island is only a memory; the cathedral suffers from the clearance which has swept away its nineteenth-century setting. The east and north elevations have lost some of their pertinence because there now seems no reason for the

height and compression which distinguishes them. The gravest
100 loss occurred when the remarkable Bishop's House, also by
Pugin, was pulled down.

15   In the frontispiece of *An Apology for the Revival of Christian
Architecture in England*, Pugin included a curious illustration of
St Chad's. There is now no way to explain the huge central
tower and spire, which, in the etching, he added to his church.
Both are out of character with the building and its proportions,
and nowhere in the plans or correspondence is there evidence
that such features were ever contemplated. They must,
presumably, be attributed to Pugin's campaign for spires in
1843.

There is much in St Chad's that is eminently worthy of consideration and admiration. The interior is impressive, even
beautiful, because Pugin managed to keep the space dominant.
The exterior is 'a mass of perforated brick walls and high roofs'
and, as Pugin wished, it consistently suggests that the meaning
of the building lies in the form and the function of its interior.
There has been general acknowledgment of the handsomeness
of the east and north sides.

St Chad's is, however, a transitional building, representing
the end of one stage of Pugin's development and the beginning
of another. It was the last deliberately dramatic interior he
would build, the last in which he would attempt to convey
his ideas primarily through an exaggeration of the proportional
relationship of height to breadth. What had begun at Derby
ended abruptly only a few months later in Birmingham.
After 1839 Pugin organized his buildings differently, as the
interior space joined with every other element of the structure
and the decoration to make a coherent composition. This
concern with totality and the ability to achieve it, which were
to be Pugin's greatest acquisitions from his admiration for and
study of medieval architecture, and the source of one of his
contributions to a Victorian Gothic revival style, had not
matured in 1839.

64

The imperfections of St Chad's are the results of indecision. Interior space is the subject of the building, and yet one perceives that Pugin was not working with that one theme only, as he had been at St Mary's, Derby, but with many. He was unsure and tentative because he had recognized that concentration on interior height produced an imitation of Gothic rather than a revival, and that it emphasized but one of the host of attributes possessed by medieval buildings.

Undecided about how he could attain his aims, Pugin was diverted by decorative details. He seems to have hoped that if there were enough of them, and if each were of high quality, a whole would somehow emerge. This explains why he made the mistake on the west front of constructing decoration rather than allowing it to decorate construction. The temptation to be ornate was impossible to resist. When he was most susceptible to the blandishments of ornament, Pugin was called upon to design the first Catholic cathedral built in England since the Reformation. For historical, religious, and ceremonial reasons, richness seemed essential. Because he wished to portray the history and character of the medieval English Church by bringing together the figures of Saints Thomas of Canterbury, Austin, Chad, Hugh, Swithin, and Wulstan, he borrowed the idea of a sculptural programme from big cathedrals and used it on the front of his small one.

St Chad's raises the question of how Pugin's buildings should be approached critically. To compare them with medieval architecture is useless, as Pugin himself found to his vast disappointment. They are Pugin, not Gothic.

Virtually every Pugin building possesses qualities of design and an originality which make it worthy of consideration as a work of art, quite independent of its place in his total artistic output. Yet separated from one another the buildings are vulnerable, for in an *œuvre* such as Pugin's, in which so many buildings were designed in so short a time and so many of those constructed have survived, the unique position of each building in the corpus of his work must be comprehended if it is to be fairly understood. Consideration of the weaknesses and immaturities apparent in St Chad's is meaningful only if the place of the cathedral in the chronology of Pugin's development is assigned its proper importance.

The Earl of Shrewsbury was in Italy on the day St Chad's was opened, but the Right Reverend Dr Wiseman – who had between the beginning of its building and its completion been made Bishop of Melipotamus, coadjutor of the Midland District, and President of Oscott College – paid tribute to the generosity which had led the Earl to contribute to 'every church erected since he came into possession of his property'. Wiseman then praised Pugin, whose 'genius and devotion' had made the 'magnificent fabric' possible. When Pugin was asked to speak at the ceremonies, he was unable to say more than a few words, and the audience perceived that he was gravely indisposed. He had been ill in February, but he had driven himself on to complete his works, although he was not fully recovered. A few months after the Birmingham occasion he was ill again, but this time he was half blind and much reduced by bleeding and the effect of the drug his doctor had prescribed, for in the 1840s mercury in large doses was considered the only remedy for iritis, no matter what its cause. Pugin was never again to be truly well.

By the year 1841, commissions in Ireland had begun to assume an important role in Pugin's practice. The chapel of St Peter's College, Wexford, was dedicated before the first stone of the church at Gorey was laid in 1840. The chapel, a big, spare building, can be identified as early Pugin because it is a larger version of St Mary's, Uttoxeter. Its bald exterior is enlivened only by a massive round window, and the proportion of its length to height resembles that of the first Pugin churches. Because it was a collegiate building, the chancel was the same height as the nave. The altar, a triptych resembling those Pugin had proposed for Derby and Uttoxeter, fortunately survives, but the screen, rood, the simple pews, and Pugin's organization of the interior furniture do not.

St Michael's, Gorey, was to develop, once its convent and satellite buildings were completed, into a work comparable in size, although not in richness, to St Giles', Cheadle, the most elaborate parish church that Pugin was ever to build. The Gorey church is large and sober, astonishing not only for its Norman style but for the ways in which it does and does not resemble the work Pugin was doing in England.

First plans for Gorey were drawn in July 1839, and the consecration took place in 1842. There are notable differences between the church and Pugin's etching of it in the frontispiece *15* of *An Apology*. Both the building and the illustration show, however, that he was following the formula he had established for the English parish church in stone. St Michael's is the direct *12* descendant of the church in Dudley. In Pugin's etching the *36, 37* front of Gorey church is shown as identical with that at Dudley. As it was completed, the former is harsh, the openings are lost in the mass of coloured stone, and the roof rises too high above the buttresses; it has little of the intimacy and character Pugin had achieved in England with a minimum of means.

The nave of St Michael's is as wide as that of St Chad's and nearly as long. Pugin appears to have kept to the proportions of the cathedral in Birmingham, for although the site at Gorey

34–35   Interior, chapel, St Peter's College, Wexford. Pugin design and basically unchanged, but screen and seating by Pugin have been removed.

36 North-west view of St Michael, the Archangel, Gorey, Wexford. Pugin had planned that the church should have a spire.

would have permitted a wider building, he maintained the relationship of width to length he had preferred in 1839. Although the basilican interior is bold and the arcade arches are low, they do not seem heavy because the mouldings are delicate and the columns slender. The wooden roof is spindly and very high. The large areas of masonry seem light-reflecting rather than massive. At the crossing, the space blossoms out into complex vistas: St Michael's is Pugin's first cruciform church. The transept and chancel, nearly one hundred feet across and twenty-six feet wide, are spatial surprises in his work. On the exterior, the size of the building, the simplicity of its masses, and the quality of its masonry can best be seen and felt at the crossing. Had the spire been built the church would have acquired the height to balance its horizontality. As it stands, with its battlemented tower, St Michael's is an understatement

38, 39
40

41

68

37   West front, St Michael, the Archangel, Gorey. The convent, also by Pugin, is to the right.

38   The nave, from the crossing to the west, St Michael's, Gorey.

rather than a declaration. Nothing, however, can detract from the power of its masonry and the clear, simple gathering of rectangular forms at the eastern end.

Pugin's Irish buildings are among the best constructed and the largest he ever produced. Robert Pierce was his builder, and much of their quality is surely due to Pierce and his masons; there was a good supply of skilled labour in Ireland and money went further there. It was the masons, working the Wicklow granite of the columns of Gorey church and building its walls, who gave Pugin's design reality. The talent, quality of mind, and feeling for architecture of the builder and his workmen were always important to Pugin, for he supplied few drawings, preferring to let the building evolve in consultation with his builder.

42   The parish churches Pugin built in Ireland, at Gorey, Tagoat,
43, 44, 46 and Barntown are akin to his English works; the church at
47   Gorey has here been related to that at Dudley, and the church in Barntown can be considered an infinitely developed and finer version of the simplest of all Pugin's designs, St Augustine's,
11   Solihull. The Irish buildings are, however, much better architecture. They are larger, but size alone does not explain their quality. The emphasis on materials, the excellence of the workmanship, the lack of ornament, the dignified and heavy proportions are more than their characteristics – they are their graces.

In Ireland Pugin was relieved of his strenuous obligation to
45   Gothic. He visited Dunbrody Abbey, and his churches in and about Wexford suggest its influence. In 1843, in a footnote to *An Apology*, Pugin carefully stated his position on revivalism in Ireland, where he found 'in the large towns, a lavish display of the vilest trash about the altars, and burlesques of classic or pointed design for churches, most costly and offensive'. He believed he knew what Ireland needed.

If the clergy and gentry of Ireland possessed one spark of real national feeling, they would revive and restore those solemn piles of buildings

39   The nave, to the crossing and sanctuary, St Michael's Gorey.

40   The crossing, St Michael's, Gorey.

41   The exterior at the crossing, St Michael's, Gorey.

which formerly covered that island of saints, and which are associated with the holiest and most honourable recollections of her history. Many of these were indeed rude and simple; but, they harmonized most perfectly with the wild and rocky localities in which they were erected. The real Irish ecclesiastical architecture might be revived at a considerably less cost than is now actually expended on the construction of monstrosities; and the ignorance and apathy of the clergy on this most important subject is truly deplorable.

For all of these reasons, the Irish churches seem now to be Pugin at his best. Twentieth-century critics who are trained to appreciate archaism, to prefer simplicity, to doubt the validity of the revival of a past style, and to set a high value on a personal and individual statement in art will find what they seek in them.

In the months between July 1835, when he completed St Marie's Grange, and the June day in 1839 when he finished the drawings for St Michael's, Gorey, Pugin had done much to advance his own career, but he had also so educated the Catholic community in England and in Ireland that it had acquired a sense of identity and pride in its history and had moved firmly out of traditionalism into the vanguard of taste. His relationship with the Earl of Shrewsbury was established and fruitful, and he had found in George Myers and Robert Pierce builders whom he could trust. The still small but promising business in the manufacture of decorative metalwork for churches was prospering under the supervision of John Hardman of Birmingham. The friendship and approbation of men such as the Honourable and Reverend George Spencer and Ambrose Phillipps were comforting. Clergy and laity accepted Pugin as an authority, whether they agreed or disagreed with his fulminations and decisions about Catholic art and architecture. In January 1840 even the Papacy expressed its gratitude for his 'exertions to promote the interests of the Catholic religion in the British capital, by assisting indefatigably in the erection of new churches both by furnishing designs for them which prove your distinguished talents, and superintending their erection'.

72

42 Parish church, Tagoat, Wexford. Originally the entire church was stone. Additions have been made at the north-east corner.

43 The nave.

44 View from the north, St Alphonsus', Barntown.

45 Dunbrody Abbey, Wexford, which Pugin visited and sought to follow in his designs for the Wexford churches.

When these early works are compared with the buildings Pugin was to design between 1840 and 1844, they seem uncertain, and more personal than Gothic. They were his first attempts to express the relationships he was convinced bound together architecture, the age in which it was produced, and his own hopes for the future of his faith. Although they superficially resembled the buildings of others who had practised and were practising in the Gothic revival style, these first Pugin churches were unusual because of his profound convictions about it. He was committed, as other architects were not, to the revival not of a style but of the verities which underlay it and of the glories and power of the medieval Church which had been embodied in its art and architecture. It was this involvement with the function of the spaces within his buildings that

46   St Alphonsus', Barntown, Wexford. The west end and south porch and elevation.

47   The nave to the east, St Alphonsus', Barntown.

distinguished him from his contemporaries, for his churches were chambers for the performance of the liturgy.

Fortunately, he set down his theory of design.

The altar and the chancel should be the first things considered in a Catholic church. However plain the rest of the structure – however limited the means of the erection – these should possess such a character as to point out at once their sacred destination.

Any estimate of Pugin's performances, his ideas and influence in his own time must include more than his architecture. He was deeply preoccupied with the meaning of the Catholic liturgy, and he earnestly attempted to restore the artistic traditions associated with its medieval setting. There is ample evidence that he regarded his work in ecclesiastical decoration as an integral part of his achievement and that his architecture developed from it. He poured energy and gift into the design of liturgical essentials – vestments, stained glass, candlesticks, furniture for the chancel, vessels, and other articles required in the service of the Mass. Practical matters, such as money and the uneducated taste of patrons, could interfere with the realization of his highest hopes in architecture; in the decorative arts, his visual memory and knowledge of and taste in medieval art could function unfettered, and his religious conviction could more easily be expressed. Architecture was a relatively new venture for Pugin; the decorative arts had been his first forte. In the year 1839 Pugin was busy attending to the works he had undertaken in 1837 and 1838. One by one the churches in Uttoxeter, Derby, and Solihull were opened as those in Macclesfield, Dudley, Manchester, Reading, Keighley, and Southport were being completed. Having begun St Chad's and various Irish buildings, Pugin was casting about for fresh projects to which he could devote himself; the first schemes for Downside College and St George's belong to these months. In a spurt of creative activity, he was to produce in 1840 the drawings for a next generation of his churches, those he was to build in Cheadle, Southwark, Stockton-on-Tees, and Liverpool.

76

49 Pugin's silver pyx for St Giles', Cheadle.

48 The silver chalice, hallmark 1849, designed by Pugin and made by John Hardman for St Marie's, Sheffield, a church by Matthew Hadfield.

At the age of twenty-seven, Pugin knew that he was no longer a tyro but an acknowledged authority from whom resounding decisions and commentary on the arts and architecture were expected, and an architect whose work was given serious critical consideration. Reviews of St Mary's, Derby, had been uniformly respectful, even reverent; one had said the church proved 'that it is not, as many appear to think, in some sort physically impossible to build real churches in the nineteenth century'.

Pugin's precipitate rise to prominence had occurred for a number of reasons, of which his talent and manifest knowledge of medieval art were two. The Pugin name had certainly been an advantage. His own persuasive ability as a designer-illustrator suggested that, given an opportunity to mature, he would one day produce buildings that were richer and more satisfactory evocations of Gothic than had hitherto been seen, for he united his spirited decorative genius, his developing architectural competence, and his understanding of and feeling for the religious purpose his buildings were created to serve. His Gothic was not applied; it was a statement of function and a reason for building.

The Gothic revival was well under way when Pugin appeared, as the long list of Gothic Commissioners churches prepared by Dr M. H. Port and the comment on earlier revivalism provided by Charles Eastlake and Henry-Russell Hitchcock well show. Pugin provided a refreshing note because he was an eloquent Catholic and talented author. His early buildings were promising, but it was his writing, his wit, and his unabashed will to educate other Catholics and anyone else who would listen that first marked him as the leader of a revival he had not begun but which he would – if only for a short time – direct, develop and modify.

CHAPTER FOUR

'True Principles', 'Contrasts'

The Articles in the Dublin Review, *and the Churches of the
years 1840–1842*

When Pugin wrote in January 1841, 'I am such a locomotive
being always flying about', he was not exaggerating, for he was
at the crest of his powers and he was aware of both his prodigious
capacity for work and the magnitude of his talent. But in his
euphoria he was expending his energy with such prodigality
that even he could not hope to maintain the pace he had set. The
ease with which he had moved into a position of power
suggested that his opponents and potential competitors had
subsided, but in fact they had not. Illness, an enemy that never
withdrew, merely waited. The year 1841 was to be one of
extravagant productivity, such as Pugin was never to know
again; it was also a year of serious illness, as the report of his
appearance at the opening of St Chad's has indicated.

At the end of January, John Weale purchased the manuscript
of a book Pugin had developed out of the lectures he had
delivered to the students at Oscott College. *The True Principles
of Pointed or Christian Architecture* was to be his best, most
original and most influential book.

The association with Oscott had been fruitful, for the
responsibility to lecture had forced Pugin to organize his ideas.
His appointment to the faculty had begun in 1837, and early in
1838 he was beginning to assemble the collection of prints and
casts of architectural details he intended to use in his classes
and for student study. 'We shall', he said, 'have a school of art
at Oscott . . . and a very interesting ecclesiastical museum . . . to
which any of the boys may have access at stated periods and
under certain regulations. I hope great things from this as I
think it will inspire the rising generation with true taste, and
make them duly appreciate the works of their Catholic
ancestors.'

The date when Pugin first drafted the text of *True Principles* is important to the history of his work because the ideas contained in the book were central to his growth as an architectural theorist, practitioner, and public figure in the world of English art. Articles which were entitled Pugin's 'First' and 'Second' Oscott lectures and said to have been written and delivered in 1838 were not published until 1846, long after he had ended his association with the college. The 'Third' lecture, which was on stained glass, had been published in 1839, before the appearance of *True Principles*. The two lectures contained in *True Principles* may thus have been 'Four' and 'Five', written in 1838 or 1839, and amended in 1840 for publication in 1841. It is, of course, possible that the content of the book was never delivered in lecture form but instead summarized conclusions Pugin had reached in the first years of teaching. It would seem that *True Principles* was written, in most of its essentials, well before its publication date of 1841 and before Dr Nicholas Wiseman became President of Oscott College in the autumn of 1840.

It is uncertain what change, if any, the arrival of the new president made in Pugin's position at the college. In an 1841 draft of his prospectus for *True Principles* Pugin described himself as 'sometime Professor of Antiquities', which could have indicated either that he had left his position there or that he taught only occasionally. In the final phases of the completion of St Chad's Pugin and the 'New Bishop' had indeed clashed over the screen; Pugin had concluded that Dr Wiseman had 'no feeling for old English antiquities and all his ideas are drawn from Modern Rome', an observation which did not bode well for their relationship. When *True Principles* appeared, however, Pugin was described on its title-page as 'Professor' at Oscott and the revised prospectus published at the same time also so entitled him. As late as 1843–6 the title followed his name when *An Apology for The Revival of Christian Architecture in England* and the second edition of the *Glossary of Ecclesiastical Ornament and Costume* were issued.

True Principles contains two separate lines of reasoning; one expresses Pugin's proselytism for the revival of the medieval style in the decorative arts and architecture in the nineteenth century, and the other concerns the abstract principles of design. It is the second of these that dominates *True Principles* and has brought Pugin enduring fame and secured a place for his book among the major nineteenth-century works on architecture.

The following principles are set forth in its text. (The page number in each case is that in the printed book.)

All ornament should consist of enrichment of the essential construction of the building (1)
In pure architecture the smallest details should have a meaning or serve a purpose (1)
Construction should vary with the material employed (1)
The external and internal appearance of an edifice should be illustrative of, and in accordance with, the purpose for which it is destined (42)

Pugin must have found ample precedents for each of these ideas in Vitruvian and other, earlier, architectural theory.

Two other observations play on the edges of Pugin's argument, but never reach the status of principles. He asserted that local and national styles and traditional forms in architecture should be respectfully considered and if possible maintained, for he said climate, cultural influences, local building materials, and native methods of construction often combined to produce structures which met the standard of his principles. And he broadened his definition of the elements necessary for quality to include social values, expressed for him through Catholicism. It was these two final points which separated Pugin from earlier theoreticians.

On the question of revivalism, the reproduction of medieval examples for nineteenth-century uses, Pugin is less definite than he was about his principles of design. He explained, for example, that even such commonplace objects as locks, hinges, and nails could be 'rich and beautiful decoration' if they were treated as 'the decoration of construction', a conclusion he had reached, he said, through study of the works of medieval craftsmen. Much as he may have wished to recommend revival of Gothic to the exclusion of all other historic styles and non-eclectic design solutions, nowhere in the text of *True Principles* did Pugin do so.

There is evidence that Pugin was aware that one of his two arguments overwhelmed and was more important than the other. After he had prepared the manuscript of the text and the illustrations of *True Principles* Pugin wrote a prospectus for his book in order that John Weale, its publisher, might advertise it and announce its publication. The manuscript of the prospectus and that of the text are in the collection of the Metropolitan Museum in New York. In this draft prospectus Pugin described the intent of his book in these words.

The present work furnishes the measure for testing architectural excellence, by setting forth the consistent principles of antient design. Hitherto architectural criticism has been little more than mere capricious opinion, and few persons could give a satisfactory reason for their approval or dislike of a Building. The laws of Architectural Composition are based on equally sound principles as those of Harmony and Grammar, and *that they can be violated with greater impunity is simply owing to their being less understood.* It is humbly hoped that this Work, which is the result of long experience and patient research, will supply in a great measure the want of *sound information* that exists on this important subject; and by explaining the *consistent principles* of Pointed Architecture, which are *inseparable from pure taste*, furnish a standard by which the excellence of the antient buildings may be duly appreciated, and the extravagances and inconsistencies of modern styles readily discerned.

Pugin prefaced this summary of his objectives with an itemized list of the principles of design he had enunciated in the book.

The following important facts are fully explained in this work.
1. that all the ornaments of true pointed edifices were merely introduced as decoration to the essential construction of these buildings
2. that the construction of pointed architecture was varied to accord with *the properties of the various materials employed* shown by antient examples of stone, timber and metal construction
3. that no features were introduced in the antient pointed edifices

which were not essential either for convenience or propriety
4. that pointed architecture is most consistent as it decorates the useful portions of buildings instead of concealing them
5. that the defects of modern architecture are principally owing to the departure from antient consistent principles.

In the year 1841, some months after the draft of the prospectus was written, *True Principles* appeared with a series of advertisements for books issued by and available from John Weale's Architectural Library bound into the back of the first edition. Pugin's prospectus was the first of these announcements. Important changes had been made in the text between the time of its composition and its publication.

Only one word in the general description of the book had been altered. Pugin had originally written that his book would furnish 'the measure for testing architectural excellence'; in the published text *measure* had been changed to *means*. There were, however, subtle and meaningful additions and modifications in the summary of the principles. Principle 1 had been changed to read 'all the ornaments of pure pointed edifices' rather than 'true pointed edifices', in possible acknowledgment of Pugin's discovery that some Gothic buildings did not conform to his principles. Rule number 4 had been revised to read '*decorates the useful portions of Buildings instead of concealing or disguising them*'. Significantly Pugin's list of principles had been increased from five to six, for the fifth principle of the prospectus became the sixth of the published list and a new rule had been inserted as point five. It read: 'The true principles of architectural proportion are only found in Pointed Edifices'.

Pugin, or perhaps Weale, had seen the implications of the text of the book and decided to avoid them by adding this testimonial to the unique excellence of medieval architecture. The important word is *only*, for if it is omitted principle number five reads quite differently. Pugin, or his publisher, appears to have trusted that readers of the book would interpret this new fifth rule as did Henry-Russell Hitchcock in his *Early Victorian Architecture* when he accepted as the central argument of *True*

Principles the recommendation of Gothic as the style to be followed, not only in principle but in actual design.

More than a defence of revivalism, *True Principles* is an exposition of the lessons to be learned from close study of medieval art. Had Pugin pursued his theories to their logical conclusion he would have been forced to acknowledge that any building, if it conformed to his principles, could be acceptable architecture, whatever its style. As was Pugin's way he had plunged into the writing of his book without considering on what shore his reasoning would leave him. His was a logical mind that he put to emotional uses. *True Principles* is reasonable and logical; the published prospectus tried to make it illogical.

True Principles contained much else. The discussions of medieval building techniques were astute and scholarly. The observations on 'modern' building and decorative arts and their failings helped to change the course of English art. The fourteen vitriolic illustrations of the sad fruits of 'debased' or unprincipled design are related to Pugin's great caricatures in *Contrasts*. The asides on scale are telling: Pugin observed that 'in pointed architecture the different details of the edifice are *multiplied with the increased scale of the building*: in classic architecture they are only magnified'. He concluded that one thing wrong with St Peter's, a building he had, by the way, never seen, was 'purely owing to the *magnifying* instead of the *multiplying* principle having been followed'. His declaration that English Gothic lacked height and that he intended to introduce it into his buildings helped to explain the proportions of his churches. Throughout the book, Pugin's distinct traditionalist bias on every subject is manifest.

An important addendum to the argument of *True Principles* is contained in a footnote on pages 7, 8 and 9, in which Pugin explained why and in what ways the Gothic of Henry VII's Chapel departed from earlier medieval excellence. The two ideas of which this note is composed show the way Pugin was to extricate himself from the indecision presented in his book. He was not going to follow where his principles led; he would

84

turn instead to a medieval authority, Durandus, and with his help justify the revival of Gothic on symbolic grounds. By saying that '*Height* or the *vertical principle*, emblematic of the Resurrection, is the very essence of Christian architecture', he was in fact modifying the rigorous doctrine he had expounded; to 'convenience, construction, and propriety', he was adding religious meaning.

Pugin was forced, on the basis of his own principles, to admit that there were Gothic styles unworthy of revival. 'From the various symptoms of decline which I have shown to have existed in the later pointed works,' he said, 'I feel convinced that Christian architecture had gone its length, and must necessarily have destroyed itself by departing from its own principles in the pursuit of novelty or it must have fallen back on its pure and antient models.' Having weighed late Gothic in the balance and found it wanting, he was himself prepared to 'fall back' to the Decorated Style in his own work. He must have taken this decision some time earlier, for the drawings for St Giles', Cheadle, had been made in September and those for St Oswald's, Liverpool, in October 1840: both churches were in the Decorated Style.

Less than a month after John Weale purchased *True Principles*, Pugin finished the text and the new illustrations for the second edition of *Contrasts*, which Charles Dolman had agreed to publish. In many ways the two books were closely related; in others, utterly different. *True Principles* is appealing and witty for constructive reasons. *Contrasts* is dogmatic, insulting to individuals and even violent.

Pugin had decided, on the basis of his experience in the years after 1836, that the worm in the Gothic rose had been not the Reformation itself but its cause, the 'decayed state of faith throughout Europe in the fifteenth century'. The English Church, therefore, had collapsed under pressure from the reformers because it was 'consumed by internal decay' and infected with – by his definition – 'Paganism'. In the cause of this new view he made extensive changes in the text of the first edition of *Contrasts*. Unfortunately, some of what he discarded had qualified and lightened the satire of the earlier book.

Pugin's new thesis was tenable; in many ways it was better informed and certainly less naïve than the assault on the Reformation which had been the theme of the first edition. It also permitted Pugin to attack the 'Old Catholics' and others who, between 1836 and 1841, had failed to accept his ideas. Those who defended 'Paganism' were charged with the blame for the enfeebled state of religion, and those who disavowed it commended for strengthening the faith. The argument also allowed him to praise Protestant societies and journals which had come forward in support of the preservation of England's medieval architectural heritage and which shared his conviction about the restoration of medieval liturgy. The issue was 'Paganism' in life and art rather than the specific faults of one church or another.

The tone of the text was distinctly disagreeable, and Charles Dolman was alarmed at it, but Pugin fought off his attempts to 'castrate' the essay by threatening to publish any deletions separately. In the end, even the remarks addressed to the Queen on the subject of Westminster Abbey appeared just as Pugin had written them: he had noted 'the apathy of royalty towards this sacred fabric. . . . We hear much of the interest certain distinguished personages take in the performances of a learned monkey, or equestrian evolutions, but small regard indeed do they pay to the resting-place of their ancestors.' He suggested that 'a visit to the neglected and desecrated pile of Westminster might teach them the instructive lesson that royalty departed is easily forgotten'.

The considerably expanded text and appendix included material on the state of medieval buildings, religion, and taste on the Continent. Pugin was indeed interested in what was happening outside of England, but his observations on these events were intended to apply to his countrymen. When he described the damage French Catholics were doing to their artistic heritage, he was, inferentially, condemning the English Catholics who laboured under 'Pagan' misconceptions in spite of his Herculean efforts to educate them. That is what he meant when he said, 'Scarcely less melancholy is it to see modern Catholics with their own hands polluting and disfiguring, by pagan emblems and theatrical trumpery the glorious structures raised by their ancestors of the faith'. He knew what he was doing, for he wrote in a letter to a friend: 'I fully await the *storm of indignation* that will fall on me when my new publications are out. The greater part of the English Catholic body are furious against me at present. Not a *Modern agitator* but an *antient one*. Had I been the former description I might have fared better'.

Little of Pugin's wilful but amusing enthusiasm of 1836 remained in 1841; he had acquired new heroes as well as new antipathies. In the writings of Durandus he had found a system of thought which coherently stated what he already believed, and an authority with whom to refute his opponents. The thirty-three books of J. B. Thiers, seventeenth-century liturgist, also agreed in content and tone with his own convictions. Pugin might have been describing himself when he wrote that Thiers' works 'display an erudition of wonderful extensive character, and powers of sarcasm under which his opponents must have writhed. . . . Though most of his attacks were made upon unauthorized innovations, it must be borne in mind that he seldom wrote, except for polemical purposes, and is therefore apt to be onesided in his representations'. Pugin termed Overbeck the 'prince of painters' and identified Giotto, Orcagna, Fra Angelico, Perugino and Raphael as ideals of Christian art. Montalembert, whom he quoted at length, and Rio figure prominently and favourably in his text. But most symptomatic of the change which had taken place was Pugin's expressed admiration for Savonarola, whose dire warnings against 'the proud luxurious spirit and feeling of Paganism' could well have served as the sub-title of *Contrasts*.

The plates were the heart of the book, as they had been in the earlier edition, and in honour of his new text he added five major sets of contrasting illustrations and a woodcut to those he retained from the first edition. The inroads of paganism could be well illustrated in sepulchral monuments and altars, subjects to which two of the new plates and the woodcut were devoted. The additional illustration on the old and new door of St Mary Overies, Southwark, is not of the quality of the rest of the material and seems to have been drawn originally for *True Principles*. Pugin chose to omit from the second edition the attack on Sir John Soane and his house; it might well have lacked point in 1841, for Soane had died and Pugin had changed his mind about the quality of the late medieval house he had, in 1836, contrasted with Soane's.

The four great plates contrasting medieval and nineteenth-century towns and the care of the poor – for which Pugin is, of all his works, best known – do not in any way fit the text, which mentions the poor only fleetingly and the condition of the nineteenth-century city not at all. Pugin had, however, been concerned about the question of charity – its character, meaning, and connections with religious belief. In 1841, at about the time he completed *Contrasts*, he read an article in *The British Critic* which pleased him immensely.

I was . . . the more delighted with what I found in the article on antient and modern ways of charity. It is one of the best if not the very best that has appeared. It must do a vast deal of good. It represents to the very letter the present state of charities among the English Catholic body. When I come down I will bring you a set of sketches I made nearly *2 years* ago to illustrate modern Catholic charities and you will perceive that there does not exist the least difference between the reviewer and myself on the subject.

The plates on charity and the city may well have been last-minute additions, prepared after the text was written and in response to the article referred to in the letter. But Pugin may also have assumed that at least some of his readers would perceive his point because *The Tablet*, a leading Catholic

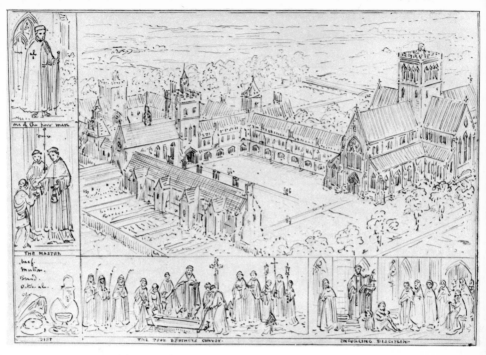

50–51 Pugin's original drawings for the plates on the care of the poor in the Middle Ages and in the 19th century, prepared for the 1841 edition of *Contrasts*. The cruciform church in No. 50 resembles the churches at Gorey and Nottingham; the scene 'Enforcing Discipline' in No. 51 was later modified.

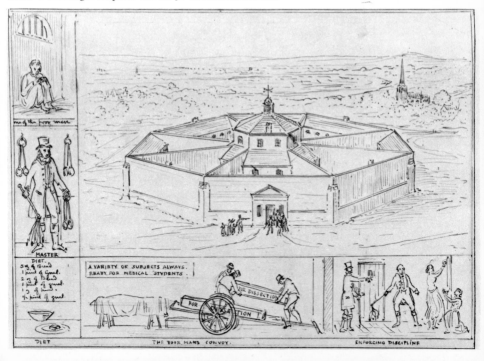

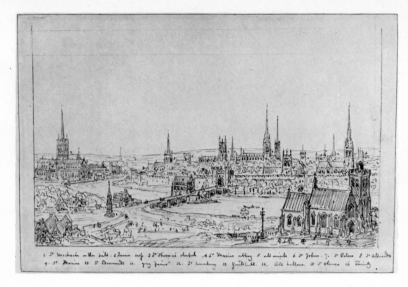

52 Pugin's original drawing for the medieval town, prepared for the 1841 edition of *Contrasts*.

periodical, had in 1840 observed (in an article which commented on the report to the House of Commons on the systems of relief for the poor in Aston and Birmingham) that the dreadful Poor Laws were 'an evil which has been rendered in great degree necessary, by the spread of pagan principles, and the destruction of the old Catholic feeling which preceded and accompanied the Reformation'.

There is even less explanation for the introduction of the plates on 'Contrasted Towns', which resemble those on charity and were surely drawn at the same time. The street scenes and episodes in the background of the architectural contrasts in the earlier edition had implied a deep concern for the character of the nineteenth-century city, but the plates had never approached the clarity, effectiveness, and decisiveness of the two new etchings.

Neither the contrast on charity nor that on towns contained a truly fresh idea, for Cobbett, Catholic historians, political theorists, and social reformers had for decades before the

90

53 Pugin's original drawing for the nineteenth-century town. In the etched version the names of several buildings were changed.

publication of *Contrasts* been calling on the conscience of England to accept responsibility for the poor and to alleviate the distresses of town life. Pugin's wit and visual acuity said more than speeches or pages could, and it is clear that he worked hard to convey a succinct and unanswerable statement of his ideas. Comparison between the nineteen buildings Pugin had proposed to mention in the captions of the drawing of the modern town – which is here illustrated in Plate 53 – and in the fifteen captions which he used in the published plate show that he simplified his earlier list and removed the names of specific persons, such as 'Pickford and Co.' and 'Messrs. Topping', before *Contrasts* was published in 1841. The drawing itself was changed in only one minor way as he transferred it to the etching plate.

These two plates, with the implied social commentary in the text of *True Principles*, were to be Pugin's only direct contributions to the pressure for social amelioration. He was no egalitarian, for he believed in government by a benign aristocracy. Chartism angered and frightened him, but he was equally opposed to irresponsible wealth and authority. His comment, made when he returned from a visit to Ireland in 1841, that 'as far as the poor people are concerned I have been greatly edified . . . [but] for the rich I can say little' was typical of his response to social issues. Pugin's battle against the 'Pagan principle' was at least in part inspired by his dismay and despair over the state of society. The remedy he recommended was a Utopia of the spirit, the Church, and the arts – a return to an earlier and, he believed, more civilized Catholic and Christian time.

True Principles and *Contrasts* must have been well in hand at the beginning of 1841, for in his letters Pugin seems to have taken them for granted. All of his enthusiasm was going into his work on an article which the *Dublin Review* would publish in May. (It subsequently formed the first part of *The Present State of Ecclesiastical Architecture in England* (1843).)

Pugin was not only aware that he was heading into a storm with the new text for *Contrasts* – he was also conscious of the power of the enemy camp, and his reasons for mounting this fresh attack on it.

I look to a *much higher standard of Catholic excellence than what any existing places furnish* and this is the front of my offence. . . . I am sure . . . that compared with antient observance and solemnity the modern externals of Catholicism are wretched, but to suit the present party a man must admire and praise Moorfields as much as Westminster Abbey and think it equally edifying but I will never compromise truth. I am ready to suffer any obloquy, any abuse, any temporal sacrifice but I will make my stand for Catholic truth and the glories of antiquity. There are a great many modern Catholics who admire Pointed architecture but they do not admire it on *true principles* as the *result of Catholic feeling*. They think Italian paganism equally handsome. Again they would apply pointed details to *modern arrangements*. This is detestable. We must have the real *spirit of Catholic churches as well as their ornaments*.

92

True Principles, the second edition of *Contrasts*, and the first *Dublin Review* article, written one on the heels of the other, illustrate well a weakness in Pugin's way of working. He was contentious, but he was no strategist. He felt too deeply about his beliefs and was too decisive to plan ahead, plot his course, lie in wait for his enemies and antagonists, or allow his ideas to mature. He let everyone know when and where he would strike, and he lashed out at persons – a fatal mistake, for in doing so he turned a battle for his admirable artistic principles and theories of Catholic art into a row. His timing was almost always unfortunate. The article in the *Dublin Review*, the third event in his campaign to educate Catholics, was as direct and clearly written as *Contrasts* was murky and ill-tempered, but the people he was attempting to reach failed to receive the constructive message of the article because they were so put off by *Contrasts*.

Instead of working his ideas out in public in three distinct but related statements, Pugin would have been better advised to write one objectively worded text, illuminated by his splendid caricatures and his persuasive illustrations. It would have been uncharacteristic, but he might have accomplished what he set out to do.

As a designer, Pugin moved with this same precipitate brilliance. If his buildings are reviewed in chronological sequence, they illustrate the soundness of his perception of design problems and his gift for solving them. Yet he worked under a serious handicap: even as his fertile architectural intelligence and talent drove him to refine his ideas and learn from experience, a compelling sense of religious obligation and a desire for perfection led him to undertake more than he could manage comfortably. As a consequence, not all of his works were equally successful.

The dramatic brevity of his career has tended to confuse assessments of his achievement. So much was accomplished in so short a time that Pugin seemed not to practise what he preached; some of his buildings failed to live up to the architectural ideas he set forth in his books because they had been designed before the book or books were written. He produced architecture so rapidly that his critics could, and did, compare one building with another without recognizing that although they were comparable in date they actually belonged to two different phases of his development. Finally, Pugin was vulnerable because of the very perceptiveness of his theoretical pronouncements; he not only judged the work of others by them but was himself judged accordingly.

The *Dublin Review* article was curiously conceived. In an unsigned review – which later appeared as the first essay in his book, *The Present State* – of his own illustration of the elevation of St Chad's Cathedral, Pugin proposed to set forth his account of the history of parish church building, the traditions associated with it, and a proposal for the designing and equipping of churches in the nineteenth century. To show that his ideas worked well in practice, he prepared twenty-odd woodcuts of plans, views, and sections of his own buildings. The article began with an attack on 'Catholic' modernism and moved on

54   Our Lady and St Wilfrid, Warwick Bridge. Woodcut by Pugin. The west front as built did not have the bottoms of the lancets stepped.

55   The sacristy and south elevation, Warwick Bridge.

to the description of the churches Pugin had built and illustrated. It ended on a weak note of apology for and explanation of the north–south orientation in St Mary's, Derby, which had been attacked in a review.

He referred to his earlier churches some of which have been described here, included several he was completing in 1840 and 1841, and introduced the public to St Giles', Cheadle, St Oswald's, Liverpool, St George's, Southwark, and St Mary's, Stockton-on-Tees, which he had designed but not yet built.

Pugin mentioned and included a view of the little church of St Mary (the dedication is actually to Our Lady and St Wilfrid) at Warwick Bridge, Cumberland, which he had designed in 1840. He could, indeed, have written his whole essay about this church, for it had every feature he declared as essential; it was the masterpiece of his Uttoxeter–Dudley manner.

Fortunately, St Mary's remains almost exactly as Pugin left it; its decoration is intact and its setting has not changed in the years since it was built. Its altar is in the east, which Pugin said was the 'antient position', according to Durandus and other authorities. It stands higher than the land about it but not aloof from it, another Pugin essential. The ground immediately surrounding the church is a graveyard; Pugin was unalterably opposed to commercial cemeteries and to churches which excluded 'the very remembrance of death . . . lest the visitors to these places might be shocked at the sight of tombs'. The west front resembled that of the church at Dudley, although *12* the latter had aisles. At St Mary's departures from and refinements in the patterns borrowed from Dudley quite change the character of the design. The central lancet is taller than those on either side, the heads are cusped and narrower in proportion to their height than were those at Dudley. The most significant additions to Pugin's pattern for small churches are the big diagonal buttresses with generous offsets and carefully designed weatherings on the front and side walls of St Mary's. On the *54* north side, there are four buttresses and the windows between

56 Sedilia, diapering, corona, holy-water vat, brush, all by Pugin. Warwick Bridge.

57 The nave roof, Warwick Bridge. The painting is original.

58 Sanctuary roof and corona, by Pugin. Warwick Bridge.

59 The sanctuary, screen, rood and pews, Warwick Bridge, all by Pugin.

them are alternately pointed lancets, and large, and composed of two lights with cusped tracery. On the south side, the porch 55 replaces one large window and buttress; otherwise the two sides are identical. The stone – dark grey with rose overtones – is local and is used throughout the area for all kinds of buildings. Pugin seems, quite suddenly about 1840, to have become sensitive to the indigenous architecture with which his buildings would live, a tendency already discussed in connection with his Irish churches.

The interior illustrates perfectly how Pugin fulfilled each of his requirements. A porch and a font are in the western end; the nave is filled with simple seats; the pulpit is next to the chancel arch and on the epistle side; and the open timber roof is painted. The chancel screen carries a rood with the Madonna and St Wilfrid, and the Crucifix between them, and the screen and rood are touched with colour and gold. The chancel is beautifully and fully appointed with sedilia, sacrarium, and an Easter sepulchre. The altar, raised above the floor of the chancel the height of a series of steps, is equipped with metal objects of Pugin's design. His two small coronas still hang on either side of it. The painting of the roof, the diapering of the walls, and the gilding of the reredos were carried out by the craftsman who was later to decorate St Giles', Cheadle. St Mary's, Warwick Bridge, ranks with the church at Brewood as one of the finest surviving examples of Pugin's English parish churches.

The first drawings for St Giles', Cheadle, St Oswald's, Liver- 60 pool and St George's, Southwark, a related group, were all 62 prepared in the autumn of 1840: the second proposal for St George's in September; the drawings for St Giles' a few weeks later; those for St Oswald's in October. More than their dates unite them; they can be seen as three variations on a single idea.

The Cheadle and Liverpool churches, which belong together, are the finest works of Pugin's early years of practice. St Oswald's was essentially a simpler and in some ways better

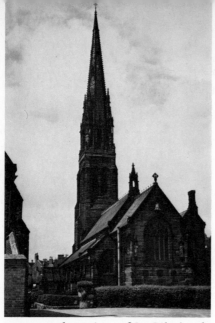

composed version of St Giles' – the significant differences being the subtle transition between the nave and aisle roofs and the greater simplicity of St Oswald's.

St George's, on the other hand, was not as effective or as handsome as the other two. It suffered because Pugin was required to put a huge building, capable of holding three thousand people, on a constricted, triangular site which was so small that it dictated the form of the church. As a result the nave of St George's was nearly three times as long as the width of its nave and aisles. The peculiarity of this proportion can readily be understood as soon as one recognizes that the nave at Southwark was over three times as long but not twice as wide as that at Cheadle. Pugin must have been thoroughly aware of the awkwardness of St George's, for when he illustrated it at the centre of the frontispiece of *An Apology*, he chose to present a bird's-eye view from the east which foreshortened the length of the nave, stressed the rich variety of the grouping in the east, and minimized the symmetrical arrangement of the front.

Having resolved to give St George's a plan of the Cheadle-Liverpool type with vastly altered proportions, Pugin was confronted with the problem of roof design for such a space.

98

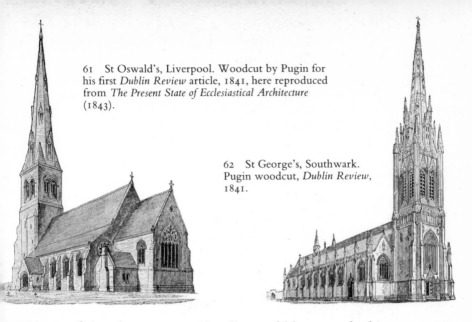

61 St Oswald's, Liverpool. Woodcut by Pugin for his first *Dublin Review* article, 1841, here reproduced from *The Present State of Ecclesiastical Architecture* (1843).

62 St George's, Southwark. Pugin woodcut, *Dublin Review*, 1841.

Aisles roofed as they were at Cheadle would have resulted in a front composed of a big tower and steep aisle roofs sloping away from it on either side – a problem he had faced without much success at Macclesfield and Derby. An arrangement in which each aisle had its own high pointed roof was an alternative that solved several problems, for on the main front the composition of tower and spire could be properly supported by a gable on either side; on the street the church could present a repetitious but dignified elevation embellished with pinnacles. The nave roof, which was bulky, disproportionate, and jarring because of its great length, could be virtually hidden from view, save from the choir end, where its massiveness would be qualified by the complex composition of the choir and satellite chapels.

Pugin's acceptance of this scheme was a compromise with but little promise. His first reaction to the site had been the correct one, for a tall central tower, a rich lower front, and a variety of forms at the crossing would have placed the bulk of the *26* building, not at the west, but squarely in the middle where it belonged. St George's became, in the end, a parish church expanded to a size sufficient for a populous urban parish, and

99

63. St Giles', Cheadle, the south aisle, nave. The gates to the chapel of the Blessed Sacrament have now been removed.

64. St Giles', Cheadle, the nave, screen, sanctuary and north aisle. The tile floor and pews are original.

the site accentuated the more cumbersome aspects of Pugin's solution. This was a case in which Pugin should have refused to build as he was told to, but the prospect of a great new London Catholic church was too enticing to resist.

As the year began, Pugin knew that later in 1841 he would write another article in which he planned to discuss cathedrals, as well as other things. He chose, however, to mention St George's in the first *Dublin Review* article, that devoted to parish church building. He said it was a 'great' church, but he classified it as a parish church; despite its size and richness he considered it part of the Cheadle pattern.

St George's, which was certainly not Pugin's best, was destroyed in the Second World War; St Oswald's, a monument of the

65   St Giles', Cheadle, the north
     buttress of the west front.

first class, has now been replaced by another and larger
building; St Giles', a church which created a stir when it was
built, remains as a positive reminder of its architect and as a
fascinating and beautiful, if somewhat puzzling testimonial to
the energy and talent that went into church building in the
nineteenth century.

Constructed between 1840 and 1846, St Giles' is, more than
Pugin's other buildings, a local product, for the Earl of
Shrewsbury, who paid for it, specified at the outset of the
project that he wished as much of the work as possible to be
carried out 'by resident artisans of the village . . . that all his
dependents should . . . be benefited by the effects of his
munificence'. Mr Denny, with whom Pugin was associated in
the works of addition and maintenance at Alton Towers, was
in charge of the building operations. George Myers, who had
worked with Pugin as far from London as Warwick Bridge,
was called in late in the building process and then only for the
carving of the most intricate stonework, such as the figures of

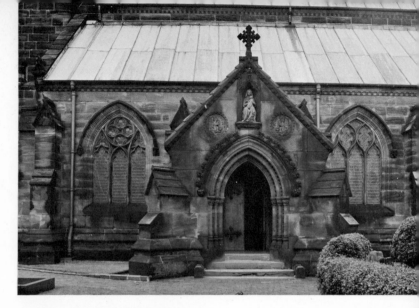

66   The south porch, St Giles', Cheadle.

St Peter and St Paul on the west front, the sculptures of the
spire, and the complex finials of the Easter Sepulchre. The
larger part of the stone for the exterior came from quarries on
the Earl's estates not far from Cheadle, as did the alabaster for
the altars. The only stone brought from a distance was that for
the piers and a fine, hard white Banbury stone used in the
sedilia and the Sepulchre. A sculptor named Roddis, working
at the site, surrounded by casts of medieval carving supplied by
Pugin, did the interior details such as the capitals of the nave.

The building at Cheadle can be followed exactly. Pugin
finished the working drawings in December 1840 and staked
out the ground in January 1841. The Earl then asked him to
move the front nearer the street and Pugin cheerfully complied.
The foundations, which had been set on a bedding of concrete,
were level with the ground by March and in June the base
courses were rising. Sometime in August, the Earl was prevailed
upon to add the Chapel of the Blessed Sacrament to the east
end of the south aisle.

At the beginning of 1842 the walls were up to the arches of
the aisle windows. The Doom painting, which had been

planned as part of the scheme from the start, was being painted in Rome, and Pugin corresponded briskly with the Earl, who was abroad, about whether the decoration of the interior should be done on canvas and applied to the walls or painted directly on the stone as Pugin recommended. To Pugin's horror, the Earl suggested a west gallery, an idea he was prevailed upon to discard when he was informed that galleries were being torn out of churches all over England.

In 1843 it became obvious that the cost of St Giles' would surpass Pugin's estimates. The Earl was also involved in the expense of building St Barnabas', Nottingham, and began to advise economies that threw Pugin into transports of grief. He wrote letters quoting the 'authorities' for every detail. The south porch, for example, was completed exactly as Pugin wanted it, although its stone roof was one of the matters about which the Earl had had second thoughts.

The design of the spire was altered and improved in 1844, and Pugin rushed about procuring casts of medieval carving to serve as models for the sculpture that would enrich it. Wailes' stained glass workshops were completing the glass, the tiles for the lower walls and the floors were being manufactured by Minton, the screen was progressing. In 1845 all that remained to be done was the decoration and the final fitting up of the interior.

As the day in 1846 approached when the church would be opened, orders for metalwork, liturgical equipment, and vestments poured into the Hardman workshops in Birmingham. The Earl would not purchase silver, so what went to his church was nearly £1,000 worth of Pugin's simplest metalwork, of 49 which only about a third was specially designed for St Giles'; the rest was drawn from Hardman's stock or made from standard patterns. For reasons of economy, Pugin chose some of his earliest designs because they were less ornate and therefore cheaper than what he was currently producing. St Giles' possesses the finest single collection of Pugin's early metal-work, exclusive of silver.

It is relevant to ask what St Giles' meant to Pugin, why he worked so intensively on it for six years, and why his enthusiasm never waned. St Giles', he said, was to be 'an English parish church restored with scrupulous fidelity', to which people might come for artistic and religious inspiration in the moment of the birth of admiration for 'Catholic antiquity'. He realized that at Cheadle, thanks to his own powers of persuasion and the Earl's wealth, he might if he persisted build a church in which all his ideas about ecclesiastical architecture and decoration and their religious significance could be realized. At long last he was to have an opportunity to compose a church which moved outward from the altar until it was beautifully and liturgically complete, even in its external details.

St Giles' was begun when the relationship between the Earl of Shrewsbury and Pugin was most sympathetic. The building they created reflects the common aim which brought patron and architect together and inspired them to continue their collaboration even when the going was not altogether smooth. The Earl was never again to undertake a project on such a scale, because his resources were later curtailed by the economic distress in Ireland, and the rigours of building this church were enough to make him think twice about beginning another. As for Pugin, by the time St Giles' was finished he was so ill that he could scarcely muster the strength to attend its opening ceremony.

The history of St Giles' provides fascinating information on Pugin's methods when he was more than usually intent upon – and believed he might obtain – what he conceived to be perfection in the whole and in every detail. In composing this building and its decoration and fittings he did not work from memory or earlier drawings of places and objects. An assiduous study of the Norfolk parish churches prepared him for the creation of the working drawings for St Giles'. The brass enrichments on the missal at Cheadle are exact copies of those on a hymnal he had seen among the treasures of the cathedral at Mayence. He bought a fourteenth-century manuscript in

67 The missal, velvet with brass mountings, St Giles', Cheadle.

order to adapt its details to the decoration of the church and accumulated casts of medieval sculpture for his workmen to copy. As he had done for St Chad's, Pugin acquired medieval objects to add to its modern appointments; the corona which *68* hangs in the chancel is a Flemish fifteenth-century original.

St Giles' emerged as more than an accumulation of accurate fragments. Pugin's scholarship and his sensitivity to medieval art are apparent in even the smallest details. His inventiveness and originality unify his diverse sources – German, French, Flemish and English – creating a whole which is his own.

In addition to the erudition and artistic intelligence he displayed at Cheadle, Pugin's fresh exploration of the possibilities of scale constituted an even more important contribution to the Gothic revival and to the development of his own style. In *True Principles*, in his discussion of scale, Pugin had perceived

that an accommodation between the size of the building and
its details was attained in medieval architecture by the multiplication of details and in 'Classic' by increase in their size rather
than number. Until he designed and built St Giles', Pugin
seems to have followed his own rule systematically; his richer
buildings, St Chad's, St Mary's, Derby, and the church at
Macclesfield, had been characterized by their feathery, small
detail which contrasted – not always effectively – with the
larger masses of the structure. At Cheadle he embarked on a
new tack, for he increased the size of the parts of the church
without an equivalent enlargement of its total dimensions.
Everything about St Giles' is somehow bigger than life: the
tower and spire are overwhelming in relation to the length of
the nave; the size of the buttresses may be seen in the south
65, 66 porch and in the view of the west front and north flank. Such
departures from the principle of 'multiplication rather than
magnification' of course permitted wide variation in the scale
of ornament, as occurs at Cheadle. When he placed the great

68   The roof of the sanctuary and the corona, St Giles', Cheadle.

69   The west doors,
St Giles', Cheadle.

gilt lions, adapted from the arms of the Earl, on the west doors,
Pugin was announcing that magnification and legible meaning
would play an important part in the design of the building.
Inside the church, large and small scale are played off against
each other. Some details, such as the lions on the corbels in the
nave, are massive; parts of the screen and the decoration of the
chancel are truly delicate. Accuracy of so many features that
had been gathered from so many places and sources, the
quantity of everything – such as the eleven splendid bosses of
the roof of the south porch, the amount of colour on the
interior, the hundreds of painted patterns each with its special
iconographic meaning – made St Giles' a showpiece of Pugin's
new conception of the revival.

The religious belief Pugin shared with his patron was suffused with emotion. Words and deeds were not enough to capture its intensity; it needed aesthetic expression, which had its outlet in buildings. St Giles' is their common statement, summarizing and illustrating the conviction of the 'antient agitators' who had so great an influence in the first years of the English Catholic revival. When their church was completed in 1846 their day had already passed, for new forces were at work which were to overwhelm their choices and preferences.

The exterior of St Giles' is heavy and emphatic, splendidly touched with sculpture and details. The interior is gorgeous: it reminds one of Victorian chromolithographs of mosaics and medieval manuscripts, and perhaps because of its blue ground, the wall of the north aisle suggests the mosaics of Ravenna, which Pugin had never seen. The response of John Henry Newman, who saw St Giles' for the first time in July 1846, is just. He was not inclined to favour Gothic, nor was he particularly fond of Pugin, but he was impressed.

The new Cheadle Church, which is to be consecrated on Sept 1, is the most splendid building I ever saw. It is coloured inside every inch in the most sumptuous way – showing how Gothic – in these countries where there is no marble, contrived to make up for mosaics, etc of the south. The windows are all beautifully stained. The Chapel of the Blessed Sacrament is, on entering, a blaze of light – and I could not help saying to myself 'Porta Coeli'. The skreens are brass and gilt wood, and thus exceedingly light – a number of paintings come from the German school at Rome. The spire is 200 feet high. Already it has cost £30,000 or £40,000.

Bestowing infinite care on every detail and allowing his tastes full rein, Pugin had created a masterpiece, opulent but disciplined. When he wrote, '*Perfect Cheadle*, Cheadle my consolation in all my afflictions', Pugin was expressing his knowledge that St Giles' was to be a rarity.

In addition to being brilliant and singular, the church was destined to be influential, for it, like St Chad's, ended one episode in the work of its architect as it ushered in another. It also suggested the way to a new adaptation of Gothic in the nineteenth-century revival of the style. When it was opened in 1846, St Giles' did not come as a surprise; from the time it was begun in 1841, architects and laymen interested in church building and ecclesiastical art had been frequent visitors to its site. The lavishness of its decoration could not be emulated, but the astonishing and original experiments with proportions and the graceful but dramatic bulkiness of the whole building invited imitation and encouraged architects to undertake less historically accurate and more personal extemporization upon Gothic themes.

In his angry pamphlet *Some Remarks on the Articles which Have Recently Appeared in the 'Rambler'*, published in 1851, Pugin included a comment on St Giles' which suggested that the decision to decorate the interior had been made without his complete agreement. He said the church had been 'originally designed for a plain parochial country church, and it was quite an afterthought of its noble founder to cover it with coloured enrichment'. He was in 1851 prepared to acknowledge that 'there is a great anomaly between the simplicity of its walls and mouldings and the intricacy of its detail'. Pugin concluded by lamenting that 'had we commenced on the same scale as we ended, a truly fine building might have been produced'. Evidently the inspiration to decorate had come from a building or project with which the Earl and Pugin had become acquainted while the church was under construction. That the illustration of the santuary at Cheadle, which Pugin published in his *Dublin Review* article of 1841, shows the walls unpainted corroborates his assertions.

The restoration of the Sainte Chapelle in Paris was under way as St Giles' was rising; the position, size, subject matter, and colour of the painting at Cheadle appear to be related to that work in progress. Pugin was in close touch with French research; his work, particularly in the decorative arts, had always possessed a distinctly French cast, and he was encouraged by developments in France in the restoration and preservation of medieval art.

St Giles' should, thus, be seen as Pugin's personal recapitulation of English architectural forms; the interior is dressed in his own version of French and English medieval painting. His taste dominated his sources; the whole was ultimately his.

The written statements about his buildings in Pugin's books and pamphlets, and his later descriptions of them showed that the preoccupations indicated in his account of St Mary's, Uttoxeter, did not change throughout his career. Although his capacities as a designer grew by leaps and bounds, and although he attained a degree of boldness and independence in his use of the style, he remained concerned with the history of the Church, its practices, liturgical requirements, the meaning of symbolism and the message of such authorities as Durandus, whose works supported his convictions about the proprieties, usages and meaning of religious art.

The illustrations that accompany his descriptions provide further insights into his ideas and methods of work. The differences between his pictures of projected buildings and their ultimate appearance require explanation. The message he wished to convey may be found in the emphasis in both the plates and the writing. The snippets of information provided in words and pictures combine to express his attitudes and to explain some of the sources of his spurt of creativity in 1840–1.

The practice of publishing illustrations of his buildings without specifying that they were still merely projects was akin to Pugin's tendency to rush into print without regard for the consequences. Accurate or not, his illustrations facilitate the comprehension of his career; his etching of the project for Downside College is, for example, all that now remains of that important scheme.

Almost invariably Pugin made extensive alterations between the preparation of an early illustration of a building and its completion. The plan of St Giles' in the *Dublin Review* in 1841 does not show the Chapel of the Blessed Sacrament, the north porch, the additional sacristy space, and an arrangement for placing the organ elsewhere than in the west end; these features were added in the course of construction. Such changes were, in fact, quite 'medieval'.

Pugin revealed a surprising carelessness about certain fundamental facts; the plan of St George's in his *Dublin Review* article shows the church to have been something over twice as long as it was wide; yet the measurements indicated in the accompanying text described it as nearly three times as long as it was wide. Nor did he trouble to redraw the plan for publication when the church was completed, even though the church had, by 1849, acquired still other dimensions. Something of the same sort occurred in the plate of the plan of St Giles', for its dimensions were also significantly altered after the woodcut was prepared. Pugin's apparent lack of concern about the proportions of his buildings, although accuracy was a necessity if people were to be guided by his standards, as he surely hoped, is disturbing. But in fact he seems to have been acutely aware of the importance of measurements; the proportions of his churches of 1838–9 differ fundamentally from those designed in 1840–2.

The earlier churches at Derby, Birmingham, and Macclesfield had been long in relation to their width. After 1840, with only a few exceptions, the ratio of length to width in all Pugin's churches falls within 12 per cent one way or the other, of a three to two relationship. When St Giles' was completed, Pugin reported that its nave was sixty feet long, the nave and aisles were forty feet wide, and the height of its bays was forty-five feet, three-quarters the length of the nave. The plan he had published in the *Dublin Review* had not had these proportions. Sometime between 1840 and 1841, presumably before the foundation was built, he had altered its proportions to achieve the three to two relationship.

These alterations in their plans affected the appearance of Pugin's buildings, making them more close-knit, concentrated,

and solid. It seems likely that he preferred these proportions
and established them unconsciously as he drew or that he saw
that they were necessary as soon as he began to prepare a north
or south elevational drawing. It is these proportions, combined
with the wide and subtle angles of the roofs, the sympathetic
treatment of materials, and the elegantly designed details, which
make a Pugin church of 1840–2 identifiable as his. Some of the
plainer churches, which did not have all of these attributes,
retained these proportions: the less successful of his buildings,
of which St George's was one, departed from them.

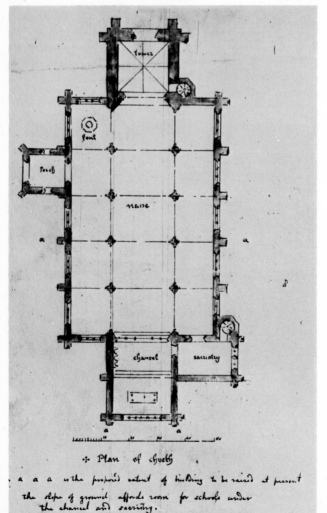

70 Ink drawing (1841–2)
by Pugin for a church,
location unknown.

The design innovations of Pugin's churches from 1840 on resulted from his new comprehension of the relationship between plan, interior space, and the encasing structure. The change in the plan was most important, but his choice of Decorated Gothic rather than Perpendicular or foreign styles enabled him to relate, rather than merely assemble, the masses and planes. As at St Oswald's, where the roofs of the aisles were 61 carefully angled to meet the starting point of the nave roof, the roofs of these new churches were less rigid and more graceful. Pugin then began to attack the problem of positioning the tower and spire; he recognized that this feature equated poorly with the rest. As the plan was consolidated, the building asserted its primacy, ornament ceased to be independent and became the decoration of construction; his increased knowledge of medieval architecture and his growing maturity and building experience helped him derive his principles and apply them in his own designs.

Pugin was largely self-educated. When he entered practice, he had at first followed where his decorative gift led – into late Gothic; his accomplishments in Derby and Birmingham were creditable, even brilliant. But his intelligence, scholarship, self-critical faculty and enthusiasm for religion and the arts did not allow him to rest on his laurels. The change that took place in his work between 1839 and 1840 cannot be accounted for solely by an expanded building budget. Pugin was moving on; he would not stop with the St Giles'-St Oswald's manner. In his churches of 1840, the last reminder of his earlier designs was the size and position of the tower. Even at Cheadle, where he took so large a step forward, Pugin was not quite ready to consider the possibility St Wilfrid's, Manchester, had offered.

St Barnabas', Nottingham, is the big English church of the Cheadle years. Its antecedents were St Michael's, Gorey, of 1839, and the church in the plans of 1840 for the Cistercian monastery of Mount St Bernard, Leicestershire. The drawings for St Barnabas' were prepared in August 1841. In January

1842, Pugin finished his second proposal for Downside and
followed it in April with the drawings for Killarney Cathedral.
The cathedral in Enniscorthy was designed in 1843. These five
buildings and one scheme which was never executed share a
cruciform plan with a central tower. All but the church at
Gorey belong to the period in which Pugin made the transition
from St Mary's, Derby, and St Chad's to St Giles'.

Three of these churches are Irish and therefore simpler than
either St Barnabas' or the design for Downside. The church at
Mount St Bernard's was comparable to those in Ireland: Pugin

meant it to be robust and vigorous but inexpensive and plain. It was not completed in Pugin's lifetime and has since been finished, though not according to his plans. Several sheets of his drawings for the monastery, dated 1840, survive; one shows the south elevation of the church he proposed.

Cruciform churches presented none of the problems of his earlier buildings. Large towers no longer dominated and upset the balance of the whole; greater massiveness and unity were now possible, without the elongation that had defeated him at St George's. He could satisfy his longing for a rich interior with crosswise vistas and complexity rather than ornament. At the east end, he could compose the soaring but poised grouping of chapels and tower that had been impossible when the nave intervened between the tower and chancel. Best of all he could indulge his preference for verticality.

Pugin could 'think big' in cruciform churches. St Barnabas' is but one-fifth longer than St Chad's, yet it seems much longer because of its division into nave, choir, chapels, and aisles. How much he wished for an opportunity to work at medieval scale can be seen in the etching of the interior of the church for Mount St Bernard's which he published with his *Dublin Review* article of February 1842. He should have known better than to print that illustration, for at that point in his career there were

72
32

72   The nave and choir, St Barnabas', Nottingham.

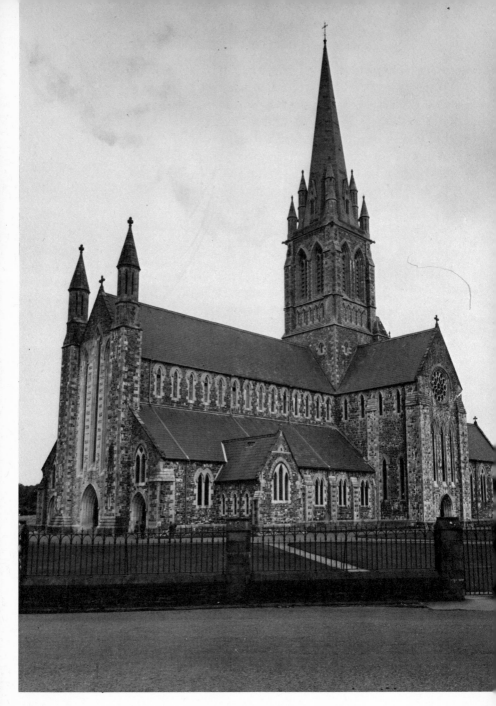

73   St Mary's Cathedral, Killarney.

many who would have been pleased to catch him in an outright distortion of fact. When discussing scale in *True Principles*, he had said the figures inserted in a drawing 'immediately convey an idea of intended size' and that 'we are accustomed to assimilate the idea of about five feet nine inches with the height of a man'. If the figures in the foreground of the etching indeed provide a measure, then Pugin was illustrating the church at Mount St Bernard's with a roof almost as high as that of the nave of Salisbury Cathedral.

He was given the opportunity to realize his dreams at Killarney and Enniscorthy. Both are stately and severe, 'rude and simple', 'massive and solemn', as Pugin had said Irish buildings should be. They are among the best ever produced from his designs.

Begun in 1842–3, building at Killarney came to a standstill in the famine years. In 1850 the cathedral was unfinished, boarded up, and part of it was being used as a chapel, when it was suggested that a drive to complete it would be a sign that troubled times had come to an end. Work began, but Pugin was not to see it completed. Edward Welby Pugin designed the reredos and altar in 1854. Along the way, changes were made in Pugin's original conception as portrayed in the frontispiece to *An Apology*. 15

The nave and aisles at Killarney are fifty feet across and eighty 74, 75 feet long. The transepts are big and the space at the crossing is memorable. Pugin did not follow the proportions he had begun to use in England by 1842, although the nave is short and wide. The aisle walls are sixty feet high and the ridge of the roof must be at least eighty feet from the nave floor. The figures in the etching of the church for Mount St Bernard's belonged in this interior.

St Aidan's, Enniscorthy, is as large as the cathedral at 76 Killarney and its site on a hill in the midst of the town is infinitely finer. The interior is as high and impressive but more graceful because of the elaborate tracery of its windows; somehow it lacks the brutal power of the building at Killarney.

74 The nave, St Mary's Cathedral, Killarney.

75 The choir, St Mary's Cathedral, Killarney. The reredos was designed by E. W. Pugin in 1854.

76 St Aidan's Cathedral, Enniscorthy. The nave and choir.

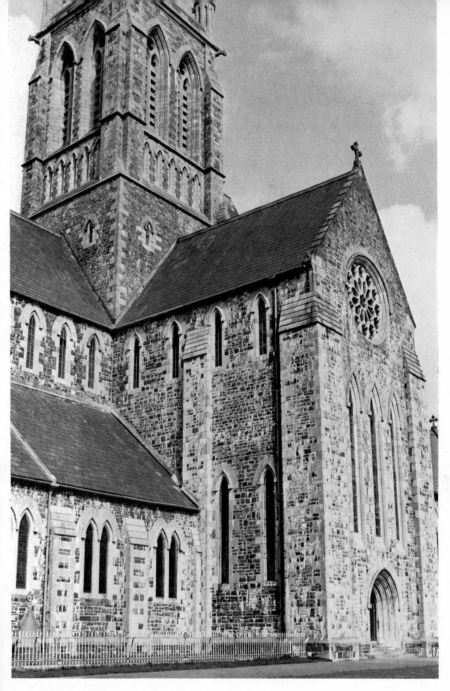

77   Exterior, south transept, St Mary's Cathedral, Killarney.

Both are effective because of 'the properties of their materials' and in neither are 'features introduced . . . which are not essential for convenience or propriety'; but it was at Killarney that Pugin's principles were most fully realized.

78 St Barnabas', Nottingham, is certainly Pugin's finest English cathedral and one of his best buildings. It is not as rich as St Giles', but it is more interesting architecture. It does not have the poise and assurance of his later churches, but its subtlety is appealing. It is not large, but it demonstrates his understanding of the potentialities of scale. It is neither innovative nor unusual, but it is sensitively fitted to its site.

The Earl of Shrewsbury had no sooner agreed to build St Giles', Cheadle, than Pugin sought his active co-operation and financial assistance in the plan to raise a great new church in Nottingham. Pugin went off to Spa, Belgium, in July 1841, to consult with the Earl and report on the various architectural projects which were progressing during the latter's prolonged residence abroad. At this meeting, he obtained the Earl's agreement to participate in the Nottingham proposal. With his usual enthusiasm, Pugin plunged into the preparation of plans when he returned from Belgium, but the scheme began to founder as soon as the Earl, who was wintering in Rome, saw the first drawings. He perceived that the building contemplated and agreed upon in July was not the one sent for his approval in December, and he correctly surmised that the design Pugin was suggesting would cost a great deal of money.

The Earl's admonitions and Pugin's violent protests reveal the reasons for the changes. The Spa scheme seems to have been another St George's, for when Pugin returned to England and took a second look at the site, he perceived that the church which had been discussed would resemble 'a mere long barn'. He must at this point have decided to attempt a cruciform church with a tower and spire at the crossing, for he said the 'sum allowed would build a compleat and far better church and one which would give general satisfaction, have a grand appearance, although *perfectly plain* and admit of a most solemn and rich interior'. In further defence of his decision, Pugin added that he had followed the pattern of the churches of Nottinghamshire and accepted the Earl's suggestion that Croxton church be the model. In a provoking and self-righteous flourish, he concluded:

Did not your Lordship say often how much you wished to see Croxton revived and is not the West end a complete revival of that simple old church with the high and *narrow* lancet windows and where was the tower of Croxton? Certainly at the junction of the transepts. I have no reason for placing the tower of Nottingham at the West end. It would be a loss, a clear loss of funds. I have *not* one tracery window, no pinnacles or any ornament externally. It will be the greatest triumph of external simplicity and internal effect yet achieved. Yet I must have *outline* and *breaks* or the building will go for nothing.

Pugin had, in this comment, described St Barnabas'. The arms of Croxton Abbey were placed in one of the windows when the church was completed.

Innumerable difficulties arose and were overcome as work progressed at Nottingham: the cost of the building was the largest of them. In 1841 Pugin had assured the Earl that the whole building, decorations and all, would cost £10,500 and that the Bishop would supply £3,500 of that sum if the Earl would contribute the rest. The first plan had called for a brick exterior, and complications arose as soon as the congregation proposed to give £1,000 for the added cost of stone. Again the Earl protested but gave in to Pugin's pleas. In the end, St Barnabas' required £15,000, of which the Earl is said to have presented £10,000. His name and his gift are recorded in the glass of the windows of the nave.

The exterior of St Barnabas' is effective, for just as Pugin had   *78, 79*
predicted, the east end gathers at the foot of the tower in a remarkable way. From the north and south sides, the nave seems long, in spite of the height of the tower which balances it. As the church is parallel to a street, one can understand why

78 East end, St Barnabas' Cathedral, Nottingham. 79 St Barnabas', Nottingham, from the north

80 The altar and crossing, north ambulatory, St Barnabas', Nottingham.

81 South ambulatory, St Barnabas', Nottingham. The wall painting and screen
have been retained.

82 The eastern chapels, St Barnabas', Nottingham.

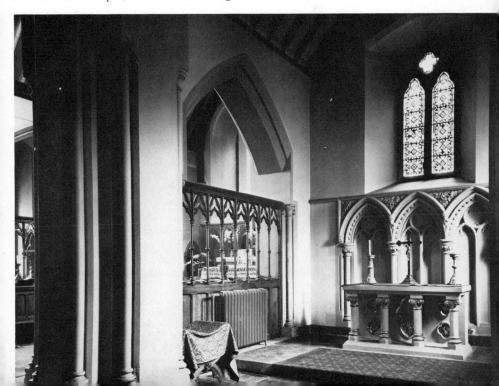

Pugin did not want to make it another long parish church, 'a mere long barn'. The nave is still the least agreeably composed portion of the building, even though its proportions conform to the relationship of width to length which has previously been described, for it is seventy-six feet long and the width of the aisles and nave is fifty-three feet.

72, 80, 81, 82 The interior has something of the quality of a miniature, a point about which *The Ecclesiologist* had a fit in its review of his buildings published in 1846. Internally as well as externally, St Barnabas' showed that Pugin had control of the situation and of his own talent, managing the space and complexity of the forms in a masterful fashion, keeping them perfectly in scale. St Barnabas' could have been pretentious, but was not; even *The Ecclesiologist* could not fault it on that score.

It is a tribute to Pugin's success at St Barnabas' that Henry-Russell Hitchcock suggests that the composition of the east end could have been studied in a model. Pugin was too impatient for models. He had a method of visualizing his buildings which would work as well; from the great seventeenth-century illustrators of Gothic, David Loggan and Wenceslaus Hollar, whose prints he collected, he had learned about both architectural styles and composition. The bird's-eye view was to stand him in good stead. More will be said of Pugin's perspectives in connection with his secular and conventual buildings.

CHAPTER FIVE

The Late Churches and Decorations

1841 to 1852

As far as his own career was concerned, Pugin's most significant comment in his first *Dublin Review* article (May 1841) was the least obvious of his remarks. Tucked away in an aside on the thorny question of churches in cramped city situations, he had said, 'Building for the sake of uniformity never entered into the ideas of the ancient designers', and added that there was ample authority in medieval architecture for a departure from the 'two and two system of modern building'.

He seems not to have noticed, or wished not to acknowledge, that all but two of his churches which he illustrated represented variations on 'the two and two system of modern building' that he disdained. What mattered in the plans of St Giles', St Oswald's, and St George's was the position of the tower, which in each stood squarely in the middle of the front. Any slight asymmetricality of these buildings lay in the eastern end, or because they had a south porch but none on the north. How little all of this qualified the symmetry of a church like St Giles' *83* was apparent in the published woodcut.

In support of his idea that uniformity was not a medieval characteristic, Pugin illustrated St Wilfrid's, Hulme, and the church he was beginning at Stockton-on-Tees. He made an observation about them which was to have enduring consequences in his own work. The beauty of medieval building lay, he said, in the naturalness which was part of '*the true spirit of* *pointed design, and until the present system of building both sides of a church exactly alike be broken up, no real good can be expected*'.

It was perhaps only human of him to have failed to mention the several very practical reasons which had led him to opt for asymmetry in Manchester. St Wilfrid's was so placed that a south porch was useless as a public entrance; one on the north

83   St Giles', Cheadle, west front.
Woodcut prepared for the first *Dublin
Review* article, 1841.

would have required that the whole church be set back from
the street the depth of the porch, which the size of the site did
not allow. A tower with a door in its base could be set in line
with the north façade. In any event, whether he had learned
his new principle of asymmetry in the hard school of experience
in Manchester or had worked it out in advance of his need to
use it there, the idea had come to stay.

Because Pugin was not alone in his advocacy of asymmetricality
in 1841, one must question whether this important and abrupt
change in his designs and theory resulted from spontaneous
evolution in his stylistic perceptions and practices or because
of external pressures. One must know what happened between
20 January 1841 – the day Pugin finished his first *Dublin Review*
article – and February 1842, when he published his second, to
know whether he plumped for asymmetricality before or after

he had become acquainted with the publications of the Cambridge Camden Society (later the Ecclesiological Society).

It seems clear that Pugin took this step alone. In April 1841, when the article in which he published illustrations of and comments on St Wilfrid's and St Mary's, Stockton-on-Tees, was already in the press, Pugin said in a letter that he had just read *A Few Words to Churchwardens*, a publication of the Cambridge Camden Society, and thought it admirable. In November 1841, he reported that he was 'delighted' with 'the last publication of the Cambridge Camden Society' – *A Few Words to Churchbuilders*, the work in which the Society had championed the cause of asymmetricality. At this same time, he was in touch with a representative of the Society, probably Benjamin Webb; Pugin said he had 'received a curious letter from a Cambridge clergyman, he is coming to see me. He has the good spirit but is evidently yet much in the dark. I trust to enlighten him.'

All of this is important not only to the question of asymmetrical designs but also to the Pugin life story and the Gothic revival. As much as the 'paganism' of English Catholics and the emergence of other Catholic architects, the Cambridge Camden Society was to be responsible for the misery of Pugin's last years.

Interest in Gothic revivalism was burgeoning in 1841. To Pugin's delight, he had found men at Oxford who were in sympathy with his ideas; at least one Roman Catholic architect, Matthew Hadfield, had begun to design buildings which could hardly be distinguished from Pugin's own. Between April and November 1841, Pugin became aware that he was no longer alone on his eminence, for he had been joined by the young Cambridge Camden Society, a Protestant group, whose position on medieval art was identical to his own. In his innocence, Pugin was overjoyed that the Society corroborated his views and that the significant literary and intellectual gifts of its leading members would be enlisted in the cause of their common ideas. So matters stood in the autumn of 1841, when

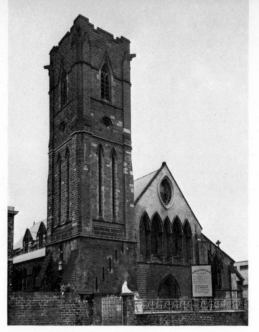

84   West front, St Mary's, Stockton-on-Tees.

he prepared the second of his *Dublin Review* articles; in it he commended the Society, agreed with its statements, and pointed out to his errant fellow Catholics how far Protestants had gone in understanding of the 'true thing'. He seems to have been unaware that his Catholicism might make him an unwelcome ally. Militant defence of medieval art and architecture was enough to bring accusation of Catholic sympathies upon the Society. Pugin, a well-known convert, was a living reminder of where admiration for medieval art and architecture might lead. But more than this Pugin had come, in his conspicuous way, to every one of the ideas and conclusions upon which the Society proposed to found its doctrinal position. He had cited Durandus in *True Principles*; he had transferred his loyalty from Perpendicular to Decorated; he had written about the English parish church as a work of art expressive of religious meaning and the history of the English faith; he had declared that asymmetricality was 'natural'. Anyone but Pugin would have realized that his days as an associate of 'the Cambridge men' were numbered. The more he tendered them his approval, the less they would like him.

Pugin meant to practise what he preached in 1841. He laid out the ground for St Mary's, Stockton-on-Tees, in the month his first *Dublin Review* article appeared. Its plan consisted of a nave and a south porch, and a north aisle, chancel, chapel, and sacristy in the east; the tower stood at the west end of the aisle, exactly where he said it should in his article. Another form for Pugin churches had come into being.

After 1841 Pugin designed eighteen English churches, one of which, a huge and complex project for Ambrose Phillipps, was never executed. In twelve of these, he placed the tower either beside the western end of the nave or in front of an aisle. In the cases where, after 1842, he did not do so there was always a good reason. The change is so definite that, if the date of the preparation of drawings in which a symmetrical front appears is unknown, and there seems no simple explanation for its appearance, then it is safe to assume that the church was designed sometime before then.

85   St John the Evangelist, Kirkham.

86   St Mary's, Brewood.   87   St Mary's, Brewood, nave and aisles.

The churches at Kirkham and Brewood were begun in 1842. 85, 86 87 Both have a large tower in the centre of the front, for they were versions of the St Giles'-St Oswald's pattern. Of the two, that at Brewood more closely resembles St Oswald's. St John the Evangelist, Kirkham, was richer than either St Oswald's or St Mary's, Brewood, and rather less graceful because the clerestory broke the line of the roof. Its interior has been cruelly modified; the floor has been lowered, the magnificent stone screen removed, and a huge altar added.

Of all his close acquaintances Pugin found Ambrose Phillipps of Grace Dieu and Garendon, Leicestershire, most congenial, for he shared Pugin's enthusiasms and violence of temperament. In 1841 and 1842, he prepared for Phillipps a lovely little book of drawings for a great house with a moat about it and a church standing nearby, which was surely a fantasy of what Garendon might become, had not Phillipps lived chronically in straitened circumstances. Although nothing came of this dream, its lineage is obvious; the church in these drawings was a combination of the general conformation of St Giles', the clerestory of Kirkham, and an east end in which the chancel and chapels each had their own gabled roof, as at St George's.

88 Ink drawing (1842) by Pugin for the church proposed to accompany his design for Garendon House.

89 St Lawrence's, Tubney.

89   The church at Tubney and the Jesus Chapel at Pontefract, illustrated in the second *Dublin Review* article, came after 1842; as neither had towers, they fell outside the compositional form being discussed here. St Lawrence's, Tubney, a small, modest building built for Protestant use, resembles Pugin's earlier churches at Warwick Bridge and Radford and is one of his best adaptations of their manner. The Jesus Chapel, now demolished, is a major Pugin loss; it was a family chapel and though very richly appointed also repeated the early parish church form. The cathedral at Northampton has been so much altered that Pugin's building has disappeared without a trace.

90   St Marie's, Liverpool, from a lithograph not by Pugin.

91   St Thomas of Canterbury, Fulham. West front.

92   St Peter's, Marlow.

All the rest of the eighteen buildings were asymmetrical; they are the churches in Marlow, Ramsgate, St Marie's, Liverpool, St Thomas of Canterbury, Fulham, Woolwich, King's Lynn (now demolished), the church at Cotton College, Salisbury, St Joseph's, St Peter Port, Guernsey, Rugby, Stockton-on-Tees, and the cathedral in Newcastle. These, along with his proposal for Ushaw College of 1840, are the descendants of St Wilfrid's, Hulme.

90–99
168

84

Thus, when Pugin discussed and illustrated St Giles', St Oswald's, and St George's in 1841, he was describing a type he was about to abandon. The question of the relationship of these three major buildings to his own later work is complicated by chronology and by Pugin's remarks in letters and published writings. St Giles' was not opened until 1846, when he was already deeply involved in his later works; its date of consecration makes it seem later in his career than was actually the case. Pugin further confused the issue because he went on to the end proclaiming St Giles' to be the 'real thing', a pronouncement undoubtedly inspired by the way he had there been able to weave together rich decoration of every sort and by his convictions about the necessity for certain appointments dictated by the liturgy. St Oswald's, on the other hand, was completed in good time and opened in 1842, after which the Cheadle style began to influence English church building, as Henry-Russell Hitchcock has pointed out in his *Early Victorian Architecture*.

133

93 St Peter's, Woolwich.

94 St Wilfrid's, Cotton College.

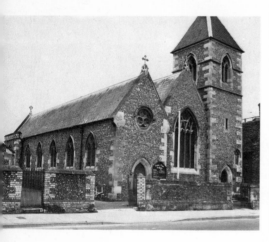

95 St Osmund's, Salisbury. The north aisle is an addition.

96 St Joseph's, St Peter Port, Guernsey.

97 St Marie's, Rugby. The A. W. Pugin church is that on the left in this view.

98–99 Cathedral Church of St Mary, Newcastle. Nave and south aisle; nave roof windows are additions.

The churches in the sequence which followed St Mary's, Stockton-on-Tees, are linked not only by their asymmetry but by their indications of still other aesthetic experiments. In his buildings of 1840, and in later ones such as the churches in Kirkham and Brewood, Pugin solved the problem of uniting the various parts of the structure in one tense and lively mass. But the big west towers still remained intractable. When he confronted the problem again, this time using asymmetrical form, his solutions were not always successful. At Fulham, Newcastle, and St Peter Port he set the tower at one side or at the end of an aisle of a three-fold arrangement like that at St George's, and the result in each case was complex and angular – a mere collection of parts. At Woolwich he put the tower at the end of an aisle of a church which in many ways resembled St Giles'. At King's Lynn the tower stood beside a church that had no aisles. The chapel at Cotton College consisted of a nave and a single aisle which ended in a west tower, as at St Mary's, Stockton-on-Tees. None of these compositions worked well because the tower somehow insisted on its independence, dominated the rest of the church, and generally confused its organization. Pugin was still intrigued with towers and spires, made separate compositions of them, and continued to treat them as additions to the body of the building.

At St Marie's, Rugby, built for Captain Hibbert of Bilton Grange and opened in 1847, Pugin proposed yet another formula for the shape of towers; his loyalty to the big, square highly enriched affairs which had filled his frontispiece to *An*

15
101
97
Apology had begun to wane. Pugin had earlier used a simple, gabled form at the convent at Cheadle and he returned to it at Rugby. The buttresses are large and projecting, far heavier than the size of the church demanded, just as the south porch at Marlow seems oversized for the nave and front. The area of unbroken and unornamented wall at the east end of the nave is conspicuously unexplained at Rugby, for the chancel does not lie in line with the nave but slightly to the north of it. In 1864 Edward Welby Pugin built the big nave and new chancel to which his father's church became an aisle and chapel. There is no evidence in the stonework to suggest that the chancel of the original church was moved in this process of addition; indeed the new building seems to have absorbed its north wall. Until it is proved otherwise St Marie's must suggest that Pugin was considering asymmetricality in his plans as well as in the placement of his towers and that he had come to share the beliefs of the ecclesiologists who had noted various irregularities in the plans of old churches and attributed symbolic significance to them.

Pugin had, in fact, found a first answer to the tower problem at St Wilfrid's and St Mary's, Stockton-on-Tees, by setting it flush with the adjacent façade. He did not return to this solution

90
until 1845 at St Marie's, Liverpool, where at last the tower joined the compact composition toward which he had been

92
moving so persistently. At St Peter's, Marlow, this difficulty is resolved; the solid sheet of its front celebrates the material of the wall, giving it precedence over ornament and announcing the creation of yet another Pugin church type.

The tendency, apparent at Marlow, to start from a solid at ground level and work upward to a separation of parts had earlier appeared in Pugin's ecclesiastical buildings such as the Bishop's House in Birmingham and in his convents and schools.

100   The Bishop's House, Birmingham (now demolished) was completed when St Chad's was opened in 1841. Woodcut for the second *Dublin Review* article, 1841. ▶

These experiments may have suggested the less scattered, more united composition and original massing which distinguished his last churches. Their simplicity, their materials, and their studied and emphatic reliance upon architectonic rather than ornamental expression all indicated that Pugin was turning for his models to the smaller, medieval parish churches, and adding idiosyncratic touches in what must surely have been a conscious exaggeration of their primitivism. The 'magnification' of St *66, 69* Giles', Cheadle, reappeared in his confident, bold management of unbroken wall surfaces and in the assertive display of undecorated building materials.

Pugin's own church of St Augustine, Ramsgate, completed *168* in the last years of his life, illustrated his understanding and awareness of the distinction of local medieval architecture, and his own feeling for local building materials. St Augustine's is a Kentish church, an observation made years ago by Sir John Summerson in an article which is one of the best on Pugin and his works. It is asymmetrical, richer in its fittings, and more refined than any of the others of its date because Pugin was his own patron. He was able to ponder each decision, supervise each step in its construction. In support of his personal concern for the building, and perhaps because they sensed his impending illness, John Hardman, George Myers, and all who assisted Pugin in building it expended their best efforts on his behalf.

These churches and the other projects of his last years show with what assurance Pugin strode from one commission to another, leaving on each the impression of his personal taste

101   The Convent, Cheadle.

and giving to each the benefit of some of the inventiveness, freedom and competence he achieved, sadly enough, just as his life was ending. Had he been able to go on and fulfil the promise of the understated authenticity and beauty of St Augustine's, to develop his feeling for and perception of the 'fitness' of indigenous architecture, and to adapt both to his late and eminently original manner, he could have retained his leadership of the Gothic revival into the second half of the nineteenth century.

As his capacities as an architect grew, so did Pugin's control of decoration. In *True Principles* he had set forth his notions of the balance between decoration and basic form. After 1841 he never let himself be carried away by his love of decoration. Even at Cheadle, where his talents as an architect and as an ornamentalist were fairly matched, the building had managed to emerge victorious from the encounter, even gaining in interest from the tension created.

On a number of occasions Pugin was called upon to rebuild, or rebuild and redecorate, medieval churches in Anglican hands. Of his works of this kind at Wymeswold, Winwick, Rampisham, Peper Harow, Beverley, and West Tofts, the first five were serious, respectful, and evocative performances. His achievement at West Tofts was more – it was brilliant; he not only rebuilt the church extensively but added a family chantry and a new chancel and decorated the interior in a style richly reminiscent of the Norfolk churches he so much admired.

The works at West Tofts were carried out between 1846 and 1852 for the members of the Sutton family of Lynford Hall, two of whom were Augustus Sutton, rector of St Mary's, and John (later Sir John) Sutton, whom Pugin had met in the early and friendly phase of his contact with the Cambridge Camden Society. John Sutton and Pugin remained in close touch with each other and together published, in 1847, a small book on the design of organs and organ cases, a special interest

138

of Sutton's. They had also shared in the decoration of the Jesus College Chapel at Cambridge, to which the work at West Tofts is stylistically related.

The rebuilding of St Mary's and its adornment was one of Pugin's finest accomplishments; the past tense is here used advisedly, for the church has been closed since the Second World War, the organ has been removed, the windows are broken, and some of the magnificent fittings have been dispersed. The great screens are still there and the sculptures on and behind the altars seem intact. The Sutton chantry is *105–110* relatively undamaged.

Pugin began to work at West Tofts in 1845–6 when he added the Sutton chantry and the tomb of Jane Mary Elizabeth Sutton and her infant son, a beautiful work with delicate and elegant stone details, executed by Myers' sculptors from Pugin's drawings. In 1849 Pugin was rebuilding the north aisle and north wall of the church. The addition of the Sutton chantry had changed the plan of the church which, when Pugin began working there, seems to have consisted of a nave and north aisle and small chancel. When he constructed the new chancel with its sacristy and organ loft and installed the Sutton chapel and tombs at the end of the north aisle, he made the plan more complex. The many drawings for the chancel and the south porch, both of which are entirely by Pugin, are dated 1850. In view of all these additions and the facts that, with the exception of those in the tower, all of the windows have nineteenth-century tracery and at least two-thirds of the walls

103   The north porch, St Mary's, Wymeswold, built in the course of restoration of the church.

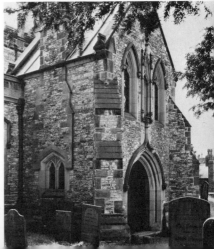

seem to be new or are so much repaired as to be new, St Mary's was in the end a Pugin building which incorporated medieval fragments. It was his largest commission for a Protestant parish church. When he died the building was unfinished; Edward Welby Pugin took over the project in 1854.

Pugin had drawn every detail of the decoration, the furniture, and the sculpture. Dozens of his drawings survive, indicating how fully he prepared his instructions for the craftsmen and suggesting how many of his drawings for his churches and other works must have perished, for the workmen at all his churches must have been as carefully directed. At West Tofts, George Myers was the builder and all the carving, both in stone and wood, was executed in his workshops; Crace supplied some of the furniture and the fabrics, cushions, and rugs; the painting of the walls and the roofs was carried out by John Hardman's corps of painters, and his firm also made the stained glass and metal fittings; the tiles, a particularly varied and interesting display, were manufactured by Minton. The colours are soft, yet glowing, and there is a good deal of white, light red, deep blue, and gold. The roof of the chancel and the painting of the organ loft are derived from manuscript illuminations and medieval examples which Pugin had studied in England and France. The paintings on the leaves of the organ blend Flemish fifteenth-century and Overbeck styles. Pugin's drawings show that the furniture of the chancel and the family pews in the nave were carved with animals – rabbits, quail, pheasants – and the plants of the neighbourhood.

111–114 St Mary's, West Tofts, ranks with Pugin's splendid Rolle chantry at Bicton of exactly the same date and with his interior decorations of the collegiate chapels at Ware and Ushaw. Together they demonstrate the control he had attained as an artist of decoration. But it is St Mary's which is most closely related to Pugin's beautiful little book, *Floriated Ornament*, published in 1849. Modestly instructive, a labour of love and refinement, this work is the most appealing of his publications and the one which presages the direction he would surely have taken had his career continued. The designs in its thirty-one plates show his feeling for natural forms and his remarkably perceptive eye for abstract design. In his simple, understated introduction, Pugin explained that on a visit to the studio of the architect Durlet in Antwerp, he had seen a beautiful capital incorporating leaf forms from plants in the architect's garden. Later, *en route* home from Antwerp, at the harbour of Le Havre, Pugin had picked up a dried thistle leaf and on studying it realized that he 'had never seen a more beautiful specimen of what we should usually term Gothic foliage'. His explanation of the principles of medieval decoration is free of references to symbolism and gently didactic. The plates and his lesson are comparable to those Owen Jones was later to publish in the *Grammar of Ornament*.

The years between 1844 and 1852 were very hard on Pugin. In August 1844, as the day for the consecration of St Barnabas', Nottingham, had approached, he had much to be grateful for; he was generally regarded as an authority, and his expenditure of energy on his art and in his battles for religious and artistic causes had been reasonably rewarded. His books, especially *The Present State of Ecclesiastical Architecture* – composed of his two articles from the *Dublin Review* – were receiving good

104   Nave and chancel, St Mary's, Wymeswold. The coronae, decoration of the chancel, the screen and the glass are by Pugin.

105   St Mary's, West Tofts, south view. The south porch, the Sutton Chantry, the chancel, are all by Pugin.

notices. Even the most haughty reviewers were paying him compliments on *True Principles*; one had said he was 'almost the only architect in England' who had seen the absurdity of practising in many styles, although he regretted Pugin's insistence on working in a dead one! His most recent book, the *Glossary of Ecclesiastical Ornament*, had been beautifully printed. The scholarship of its text had begun to enhance his reputation and establish him as something more than an architectural and religious polemicist. His practice was prospering: he had been called upon to design for two Oxford colleges, Magdalen and Balliol; he had laid the foundation stone for a large new work at Alton, a castle to stand near St John's hospital; churches continued to come his way and he was beginning a number of new conventual establishments; various gentlemen had retained him to embellish their properties or renovate their houses; and he was building a new house for himself and his family – which he said was to be a 'folio edition of St Marie's Grange' – on a splendid site overlooking the sea near Ramsgate.

106 Bosses and painting, undersurface of the Sutton Tomb, Sutton Chantry, St Mary's, West Tofts.

107 The organ loft, the chancel, St Mary's, West Tofts. The wall painting, roof painting, furniture, are by Pugin.

108　The chancel, St Mary's, West Tofts. The screen, tiles, furniture and architectural sculpture in stone are all by Pugin.

109　The painted roof, the Sutton Chapel, St Mary's, West Tofts.

110　East end of the north aisle, St Mary's, West Tofts. The Sutton Chapel. Screens, glass, carved altar (concealed) are all by Pugin.

In decorating and furnishing it, he had the co-operation of J. G. Crace who, with Myers, Hardman, and Minton, was to complete the coterie of men with whom he worked most often and best.

At the same time Pugin was called upon to face problems he had not previously known and to take criticism of the kind he had been meting out to others. He suffered the saddest disappointment of his professional life in 1843–4 when his proposal for Balliol College was rejected because he was a *115* Catholic. Pugin had found the order for the plans for a new

143

111 The Rolle Chantry, Bicton. The building and decorations are by Pugin, the arcade is a fragment from the old church, somewhat restored.

112 The Tomb of Lord Rolle, the Rolle Chantry, Bicton. Pugin's sculpture and tiles.

113 The painted roof, the Rolle Chantry, Bicton, design by Pugin.

114 The brass lectern, Ushaw College, design by Pugin.

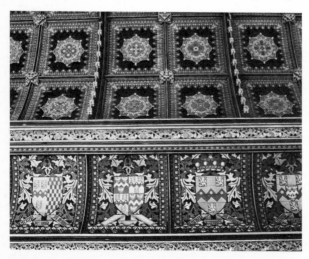

college 'almost too exciting to bear'; he worked so hard on them that he was 'overcome' when they were finished and 'could scarcely sleep while the designs were in hand'. That in the tense atmosphere of Oxford he should meet with the disapproval of the President and Fellows seemed no more than an expected personal injustice. It was the design for which he grieved; Pugin was sufficiently objective to recognize that he had given the college the best work of his career.

People had begun to fight back in response to his attacks. *The Builder* had rushed to the defence of J. J. Scoles, whom Pugin had condemned in *The Present State*. *Punch* amused itself at his expense by publishing a very funny and astute illustration and discussion of how, following Pugin's principles, the façade of the British Museum might be made expressive of its purpose, and later a series of lampoons on the Houses of *116, 117* Parliament and on Pugin as the champion of the medieval cause in art.

115   One of the 1843 drawings submitted to Balliol College as Pugin's proposal for its rebuilding.

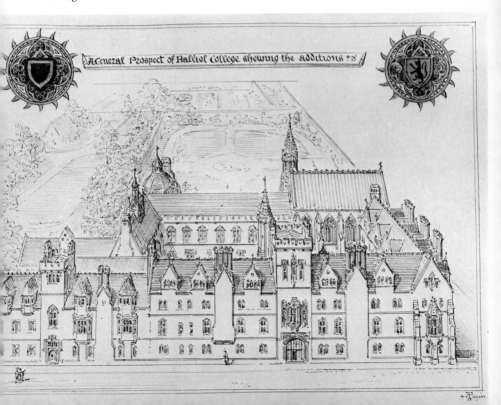

Perhaps the greatest disappointment occurred in his relationship to the translators and editors of Durandus. In their long introduction to the translation of the *Rationale divinorum officiorum,* John Mason Neale and Benjamin Webb, leaders of the Cambridge Camden Society, criticized Pugin harshly. To everyone but Pugin the reason for the assault on his reputation and artistic integrity must have been obvious, for the Society proposed to lay claim to many of the ideas he had earlier enunciated. To Pugin this turn of events was inexplicable, however, and his feelings were injured. 'There is a most interesting translation of *Durandus* coming out with an introduction on Symbolism, which is admirable', he said, but he added,

to my great grief I am mentioned as a *Schismatick* and this is the only matter in the whole work that is not quite in the true spirit and I am the more grieved at it because it is *Lugged* in without any cause and they might have left me out altogether, indeed I am sadly misrepresented in what they say for they accuse *me of being indifferent to Symbolism in architecture* ! ! ! after all I have written and done this is too bad, and the introduction is written by two Camden men whom I greatly respect.

FOR PARLIAMENT.

In 1843–4 Pugin for the first time found himself competing with other architects and designers in the decorative arts who were determined to share in Catholic building. He approved of Matthew Hadfield but found Charles Hansom less agreeable. Pugin's buildings were believed to be costly; he had been working for a rich man and his early experiments with revivalism had been expensive, more because of his high standards than because of his immaturity. In spite of his excellent reputation as an artist, Pugin had not been accommodating to his clients. He had built enough to provide others with models, and from this point on he was to be but one of several employed in his chosen field.

His personal life seemed hopeful and happy, in spite of these mounting external pressures. Mrs Pugin had become a convert to Catholicism and so shared his enthusiasms. The family had settled in Chelsea after leaving St Marie's Grange, and they lived in a house which stood, Pugin said, on ground which had once been Sir Thomas More's garden. For the sake of the children and the pleasures of the seaside, which both Pugin and his wife enjoyed, they all moved to Ramsgate for many weeks of each year. There had been three children when the Pugins left Salisbury; by 1844 there were six. Anne was twelve, Edward Welby eleven, and Agnes seven. Cuthbert, age four, Katherine, two, and the baby Mary, who was nearly a year old, had been born in London or Ramsgate.

After the dreadful illness of 1841, during which he had nearly lost his sight and had been heavily dosed with mercury, Pugin had remained well. Save for one mild attack of influenza in 1842, he had been perfectly healthy and his constitution seemed able to stand up to the incessant travel and hours of work he demanded of himself.

In August 1844, he was completing the last details of the church in Nottingham, beginning his work at the castle in Alton, tending to the decorations and building at Ushaw College, and working on St Giles', Cheadle. He was at Alton when he received an urgent message to return to London, for

◀ 116–117   Two attacks on Pugin, one for his work in the decoration of the Houses of Parliament, the other lampooning his ideas, his repetitive use of his initials and motto *En Avant* (*Punch*, 1845, pp. 150, 238).

his wife was seriously ill; on 22 August, Louisa Pugin died. Her body was sent to Birmingham on the 25th, and with Edward Welby, who was inconsolable, Pugin left to be present at the consecration of St Barnabas'. On 30 August, the two attended the funeral at St Chad's, Birmingham, and that night they returned to London, where Pugin began the process of moving his family to the new house in Ramsgate.

It was in 1844, a matter of weeks after Louisa's death, that Charles Barry sought Pugin out and asked for his further assistance in the interior decoration of the Houses of Parliament. Pugin accepted. His architectural practice was in transition, and although he had plenty to do, he was sure everything was collapsing about his ears. His household was in confusion. A marriage proposal he had made had not been favourably received. He was ill and haunted by sorrow over his wife's death. Nevertheless, his business in metalwork was extremely prosperous and he had so much to do that he complained constantly. He and Hardman had decided to begin to manufacture stained glass themselves, because Pugin had had nothing but difficulties and irritation in his relationships with his three former craftsmen, and the new Pugin–Hardman venture had met with instantaneous success.

It is against this background that the achievement of Pugin's last years must be seen. He was ill much of the time, afflicted with iritis, and being given so much mercury that he suffered from the effects of the drug as much as from the disease it was supposed to cure.

A further and truly damaging critique of his work appeared in *The Ecclesiologist* in 1846, at a time when Pugin was ill with kidney disease and burdened with innumerable orders for designs for the Houses of Parliament, for stained glass windows, and for furniture and metalwork. He was further harassed because he was too ill to visit his buildings in progress. The final blow came when he realized that he, Ambrose Phillipps, and the Earl of Shrewsbury were losing ground as leaders of Catholic taste. On an ill-starred day in 1848, Phillipps and Pugin visited the Reverend Father Frederick Faber (who was later to be associated with the Brompton Oratory) at St Wilfrid's, Cotton. There was a scene over screens, the repercussions of which were to travel far. Phillipps and Faber seem to have been the chief participants in the argument, but Pugin's ideas were at stake and his hopes can only have been dashed by what he heard. He was not accustomed to losing battles, and now he was destined to meet defeat in a matter closest to him.

118 An 1845 pencil drawing with two portrait sketches of Louisa and the youngest Pugin child.

119–120 The Convent of the Sisters of Mercy, Alton. The part of the building to the left of that in Plate 120. The Convent, Alton, the building originally called St John's Hospital; the western front of the group.

121 The Church of St John, Baptist, Alton, a view continuing that in Plate 120.

122 The Convent of the Sisters of Mercy and the Church of St John, Baptist, Alton; the east end of the church, the north wall of the convent.

CHAPTER SIX

Convents, Monasteries and Schools

Smaller Domestic Architecture, 1835 to 1852

The task of designing, building, and equipping churches seemed to Pugin the essential part of his practice and his first obligation, but he was also eager to create a public demand for suitable and dignified auxiliary ecclesiastical buildings, such as convents, monasteries, schools, episcopal residences, and presbyteries. As he was often called upon to execute work of this kind to accompany his churches or to house Catholic institutions, he had ample opportunity to develop his ideas and to evolve a positive and individual style in such structures.

Pugin's buildings of this sort are often singularly instructive, and always personal. Although they resemble one another, they are, as a group, quietly original. He felt free to treat them simply and casually, for they did not elicit, as did his churches, a respectful and conservative response. Convents, schools, and presbyteries were often relatively inexpensive and intended to be inconspicuous and serviceable. Pugin treated them very much as he did his smaller houses. He had a knack for informal domestic architecture; the results were invariably effectively composed and comfortable. The same can be said of his conventual, institutional, and residential ecclesiastical architecture.

Over the years Pugin designed a significant number of buildings of this kind – more than the number of churches. The drawings for the convent in Bermondsey, his first, were made in 1838. The Bishop's House in Birmingham, St John's Hospital, Alton, and a first scheme for Downside, too big and too elaborate to be practical, were all designed in the late summer of 1839, immediately after the plans for St Chad's and for the church at Gorey. Mount St Bernard's Abbey and the convent in Birmingham followed in 1840, the year of St Giles', St

100

119–122

123–126

123 Mount St Bernard's Abbey, the cloister built according to Pugin's original design.

124 The Convent of Mercy, Handsworth, Birmingham, from the cloister. The building with stone dressings is not by A. W. Pugin; the chapel on the immediate right is a reconstruction after bomb damage in World War II; the brick structure with the tower is part of the original Pugin design.

125 The Convent of Mercy, Handsworth, Birmingham. The cloister.

126 The street front of the Convent of Mercy, Handsworth, Birmingham. John Hardman's residence, on the extreme right, was also added to by Pugin.

127 Convent of the Presentation, Waterford, side elevation.

Oswald's, and St George's, each of which had its own complement of residential, educational, and conventual buildings. The convent in Waterford, his finest conventual design, and the highly effective block at Ratcliffe College belong to Pugin's greatest year, 1841. So do the second Downside proposal – that illustrated in the 1841 *Dublin Review* article – and St Barnabas', Nottingham. The convent in Liverpool was begun in 1842, and there are others in Gorey and Birr in Ireland and in Nottingham. Nor does this exhaust the list; the convents at Cheadle and Southwark have been alluded to, and there were, as well, dozens of presbyteries and small schools.

130

101

128–129 Chapel of the Convent of the Presentation, Waterford; details of the screen and furniture.

130   Ratcliffe College, Leicestershire. Pugin designed the main entrance and tower
and the wing to the right of it. The rest of the quadrangle composing the present
college are later additions in his manner.

This chronology has a pattern similar to that of his church
practice: accelerated growth, a sudden series of masterpieces
in 1841 and 1842, and less work after 1844. There the similarity
ends, for in his domestic, conventual, and institutional architecture, there is no equivalent to the change to asymmetricality
in his churches. An abrupt alteration in the pattern was
unnecessary. Because he was not hampered by precedents,
traditions, and emotional and religious involvement in this
sort of building, Pugin had early begun to work in two positive manners and he kept to them, refining as he went along.
He had found one before 1835 and the other in 1835, between
the first and second designs for St Marie's Grange.

In 1833, as he was training himself to be an architect, Pugin
has set imaginary design problems for himself which he worked
out in complete detail. His letters to E.J. Willson indicate that
he had sought criticism and advice on these studies. Pugin

131 The Convent of Mercy,
Mount Vernon Street, Liverpool.

seems to have carried the drawings about with him as evidence of his skill; they could well have convinced Charles Barry to hire him to assist on the Birmingham school interiors and fittings in 1835. Of his several exercises of this kind, Pugin was particularly attached to one, a little volume of drawings for a Deanery which he had in his imagination situated in the Close at Salisbury. One of his last acts before his collapse and death in 1852 was to ask that the book be returned by a friend who had borrowed it. A version of the Deanery building from this group of drawings appeared in *True Principles* – much simplified and stripped of its ornament and accompanied by a large church – where Pugin entitled it an 'Old English Mansion'.

The Deanery of the drawings was too richly ornamented ever to be built in all its details, but it was, in general, to become the basis of his stone conventual and domestic architectural designs. Scarisbrick Hall developed from it, as did the Hospital at Alton, and the drawings for Balliol College are its finest expression.

Pugin's alteration of his conception of St Marie's Grange in 1835, from the French affectations of his first idea to something much plainer and somehow more English, suggests that he had found a model which pleased him. At the sale of his 'framed engravings, drawings and paintings' in 1853, a group of Hollars turned up, among them a number of the London views, including that of the Waterhouse at Islington and the 'Long View of Greenwich'. Few prints or drawings are the shape of the view of Greenwich, which is composed of two long narrow prints, each six by a little over sixteen inches. The framed pictures that appear over the entrance to the chapel in Pugin's watercolour of St Marie's Grange resemble them in shape and in the location of the dark and light areas in the views. The irregular and picturesque roof of the old observatory and the height and massing of the Islington Waterhouse as Hollar rendered them suggest that it was he who provided Pugin with the fresh inspiration for his house.

132–134

3

132-133   *The Long View of Greenwich*, by W. Hollar.

That Hollar's architectural and topographical prints supplied
Pugin with seminal ideas and models for his own style of
illustration is borne out by a comparison of Hollar's view of the
interior of Westminster Abbey and others of his prints of
Gothic architecture and Pugin's etching of St Mary's, Derby.
In addition to his collection of framed Hollars, Pugin owned a
beautiful copy of Dugdale which possessed its full complement
of the Hollar illustrations.

18

From his citation of sources in *Contrasts*, it becomes clear that
Pugin used sixteenth-century commentators and historians,
such as John Stow, to form his image of the pre-Reformation
world. The works of Hollar offered pictures of that world, for
his prints contained not only sensitive and sympathetic

134   *The Islington Waterhouse*, by W. Hollar.

evocations of major and minor Gothic monuments but views of the secular architecture of the late Middle Ages which remained in seventeenth-century London. Pugin owned Hollar's 'Large Prospect of London from Lambeth', and it is rewarding to compare his secular and conventual architecture with the buildings in the foreground of this print.

Pugin's library contained hundreds of seventeenth-century imprints, many with illustrations of medieval architecture. He had the *Topographiae Europae* and *Topographiae Galliae* by the Merians, comprising twenty volumes of views of cities in which, although the scale is small, details of buildings, and their general massing, arrangement of chimneys, and pitch of roofs are perfectly legible. Pictures of cities seem to have pleased Pugin; when he moved to Ramsgate in 1844, he had a large view of Bruges framed to hang in his library-drawing office. He was also a collector of maps, some of which included bird's-eye views of cities in their margins.

The bird's-eye view was the special pleasure of Baroque book illustrators who developed its potentialities with great virtuosity. Pugin owned Loggan's *Oxonia et Cantabridgia Depicta* and mentioned it in his letters; there can be little doubt that Loggan and other seventeenth-century sources were responsible for the bird's-eye views which he used so often. *True Principles, Contrasts* (the 1841 edition), *The Present State*, and his volumes of drawings for projects are rich with them.

The last great illustrators of Gothic, until the Pugins came along, had lived in the seventeenth century. The quantity and quality of this kind of material in Baroque books is astonishing. That a great Gothic revival architect who was also a scholar and a connoisseur of draughtsmanship and the history of illustration and printing should have found the Merians is not surprising, especially as Pugin had early begun to collect the works of Hollar.

In *Some Remarks on the Articles Which Have Appeared in the 'Rambler'*, Pugin described his progress into the past.

The seven sacraments of the Church I found on many a sculptured front, and the vestments on the priestly effigies set forth the splendour of the ancient solemnities. By the help of the histories of the devout and painful Dugdale I replenished, in imagination, the empty sacristies of York and Lincoln with a costly array of precious vessels and reliquaries and richly embroidered imagery, and I could almost realize the Venerable Hugh celebrating in the glorious choir which he had raised.

Paul Frankl has said that 'the *Monasticon Anglicanum* became the first illustrated history of a medieval style, although the text dealing with its purely artistic side still remained to be written'. Pugin did not require such a text: he could supply it for himself. Dugdale's account reinforced his view of the greatness of the Middle Ages and of the scale of the disaster brought on by the Reformation. He found Hollar's views in perfect accord with his own sensitive drawing style and taste in subjects, for the early master too had enjoyed the boats on the Thames and the delicate interweaving of vaults.

Pugin's reference to these sources in no way qualifies the originality of his own achievement. Rather, it indicates how his mind and eye worked, how scholarly were his interests, and yet how alive and imaginative his feeling for the history and practice of the arts remained. He learned from Hollar as one might from a master; Pugin can be said to have served his apprenticeship under him. He did not copy the buildings Hollar and Merian had illustrated; he perceived their characteristics and came to understand the relationship between their parts, their proportions and their relationship to each other in an urban setting. There was, of course, a risk that Pugin might perpetuate in his buildings details which derived from the illustrator's manner rather than from his architectural subjects. Some Pugin buildings do preserve mannerisms that are part of Hollar's drawing style; St Marie's Grange is rather attenuated, and the school at Spetchley verges on quaintness. But by and large when he was working in his best form, as at the Bishop's House in Birmingham and at his own house, The Grange, Ramsgate, only Hollar's lessons, not his details, influenced him.

Pugin rarely succumbed to the temptation to follow foreign models for buildings in England, despite his use of such sources as the Merians and his frequent travels and sketching on the Continent. The castle at Alton seems to be derived from German 137-139 and French examples, yet its details and the fundamental simplicity of the exterior and interior are English. The alien style of St Chad's was unique in his practice. His belief that nineteenth-century architecture should resemble the local building with which it would be associated – a point he made about his Irish works – stood him in good stead, for it restrained him from using foreign forms in an English setting and curbed his enthusiasm for the richly ornamental. So closely do his buildings sometimes conform to local practice that, in cases

135 School at Spetchley, Worcestershire.

such as the lovely Glebe Farm in Rampisham, it is almost impossible to recognize that they are of the nineteenth century and are the work of an architect rather than a local mason builder of the fifteen or sixteenth century.

Pugin's second style in secular and auxiliary ecclesiastical works is, therefore, the one he derived from study of Hollar and Merian and adapted until it became his own. It begins with St Marie's Grange and runs throughout his career. All of the brick convents – those in Birmingham, Nottingham, Liverpool *130* – the institutional buildings such as Ratcliffe College, innumer-*140* able small houses, and one of his churches, that at Kenilworth, belong to it.

The distinction between Pugin's brick style and the Deanery manner he used when working in stone lies in the additive nature of the former. Nowhere can this characteristic be seen to better advantage than in the Bishop's House in Birmingham, the first building in which Pugin attained mature expression of this method. The parts of the house tend to become smaller as the structure rises from the ground. The windows are distributed asymmetrically, and their positions bespeak the nature of the plan. The chimneys are prominent, forming tall buttresses and serving as decorative patterns against the walls. The angles of the roofs are acute, and they merge with and emerge from one another exactly as the plan dictates. The total effect is of an accumulation of masses rather than a block in which openings have been drilled. The portrait of Winchester

160

137　The vaulted roof of the chapel, the Castle, Alton.

138　The Castle, Alton. Its relationship to the Convent of Mercy is apparent in Plate 122. The living quarters are in the main block.

139　The interior of the chapel in the Castle, Alton.

House in Hollar's view of London from Bankside suggests the source of many of the details of the Bishop's House, but it cannot account for the coherence and continuity of the whole.

Many of these brick buildings tended, if the site suggested it, to be complex in plan and to ramble, fitting themselves to the ground on which they stood. The illustration of the Convent of Our Lady in Birmingham, which Pugin published in 1842, showed no accommodation to the distinct slope of the site; when the building was completed the cloister had been arranged to step down the hill. The small scale and informality without fragmentation that Pugin could attain when he worked with

125

141 brick can be seen in St Anne's Bedehouses in Lincoln, where he provided the drawings but neither saw the site nor supervised the construction. George Myers built from the drawings Pugin gave him without the benefit of the advice and emendations normally provided in the course of collaborative construction. The result is an unmodified Pugin conception in which all of the traits of informality, smallness of scale, and exaggerated medievalism may be seen in their most primitive form.

In the early years of Pugin's career, there was little interaction between his church designs and his secular works. Until the construction of the Bishop's House in Birmingham, such influence as there was ran from the churches to the secular works, with the result that the houses on either side of the front 17 of St Mary's, Derby, in Pugin's etching are made to harmonize with the church. Between 1839 and 1841, a new kind of 100, 124, 125 reciprocal relationship begins to appear. At the Bishop's House, and again at the convent in Birmingham, Pugin had united the parts at ground level and gradually separated them as they rose, an intimation of an organization that would 92 receive emphatic expression in the west wall of St Peter's Marlow. Even in his last works, Pugin was experimenting; discoveries made in secular building appear in his church designs.

In the end this brick style became a formula, as the illustrations in *The Present State* well show. Given a convent to design, Pugin would arrange the blocks around a cloister, depart from the rectangular form with the positioning of the chapel, and let the chimneys and a few buttresses vary the façades. He

140
St Augustine's,
Kenilworth.

141 St Anne's Bedehouses, Lincoln.

142 Convent, Birr, County Offaly. The larger part of this building was completed by E. W. Pugin. The main front resembles the A. W. Pugin design.

satisfied every functional requirement in as simple and direct a manner as possible. When he was engaged to build the convent in Birr, the Irish *Catholic Directory* published a drawing of his proposal, which, even had it not been attributed to him, would have been perfectly recognizable as his; it was a bird's-eye view of a severe, heavy, stone version of the Birmingham and Liverpool convents.

Works such as these would never astonish, for like St Wilfrid's, Hulme, they were almost commonplace. They were new, however, because Pugin was, at last, designing not 'a compleat building of the fifteenth century'; he was designing according to fifteenth-century principles.

The Grange at Ramsgate, which Pugin built in 1843 and 1844 *143* as a home for his family, offers ample evidence of the maturity he attained after 1841–2. It was neither a cottage nor a mansion but a spacious and unostentatious residence in which Pugin was clearly at ease with the style he had evolved from study of medieval buildings, illustrations of them, and his own liberating discovery that architectural principles could take precedence over careful revivalism. The Grange was not Gothic, but it could never have been conceived without Pugin's knowledge of medieval domestic architecture. It was not eccentric, but it was unusual in its pleasant sturdiness, which had been derived from a clear intention and willingness to experiment. The house must have been well known, for Ramsgate was a popular seaside resort in the nineteenth century, and visitors to the Sands were surely aware of the Pugin compound on the cliff.

In order to understand Pugin's building, it is necessary to relieve the Grange of the additions which have since been made to it. After Pugin's death, Edward Welby Pugin, Mrs Pugin, and Cuthbert Pugin maintained the house as their principal residence throughout their lives. In the course of time, changes were made by the brothers. A long glazed entry way was added on the street front. A greenhouse and an addition to the drawing room were placed on the west end of the ground floor; the former has since been removed. The kitchen and service quarters were rebuilt and increased in size and complexity. The outbuilding which forms part of the wall along the road was completely rebuilt by E. W. Pugin. And there are indications that the chimneys, roofs, and dormers of the main house were also extensively reconstructed or repaired at some time.

Pugin had built a house that was simple, dignified, and comfortable. On the exterior, the severity of its brick walls was qualified only by the stone dressings around the windows and doors and by the oriel on the sea front, which opened into the library and the master bedroom above it.

The Grange is set back from the road the depth of a courtyard. It presents a U-shaped front on that side, the arm on the left being longer than the one on the right. The wing on the right projects but a few feet from the main east–west block,

143   Proof of an etching by Pugin, 1848, showing the Grange, Ramsgate, before the construction of St Augustine's.

144   The Grange, Ramsgate, view of a portion of the courtyard façade.

and its only adornments are its asymmetrical design and the chimney of the drawing room which is corbelled from it. On the left the kitchen and service wing comes further forward, terminating in an unusual triangular form, the cluster of chimneys so arranged to converge at its apex. The main door – now hidden by the entry passage – is in the rear wall of the U, and beside and above it the large window of the hall and staircase rises on the left. Most of the simple elegance of this front has been obscured or confused by the additions which have been mentioned above.

The façade on the sea is equally understated; only the slight recession of the tower and the oriel vary its lines. The elevation is, however, irregular, because of the break in its roof line caused by the gable which runs from front to back, intersects the lengthwise roof, and emerges above the oriel. In the end, the effect of the Grange depended upon the conformation of its roofs, the simplicity of its masses, and the frank use of its building materials. There were no features about it that were not 'necessary for convenience, construction or propriety'.

The interior is as successful as the exterior. Pugin himself must have been pleased with it, for he repeated the plan at the *136* Glebe, Rampisham, and at the parsonage at Lanteglos, near Camelford. The house at Wilburton, Cambridgeshire, attributed to Pugin, has the same interior, which appears yet again *148* in Mr Sharples' elaborate mansion in the outskirts of Liverpool. Finally, the entrance hall at Burton Close, near Bakewell, suggests by its resemblance to the hall of the Grange that Pugin may have had a part in its design.

The Grange must in its time have been a livable house. The service areas were close to, but separated from the family apartments. The dining and living rooms looked out upon the sea, and the decorations of walls and fireplaces were carefully scaled to the height of the ceilings. Stained glass in the windows provided a discreet suggestion of medieval richness and colour. The tiles of the hall floor announced the owner's lineage. But it was the tall, two-storey hall which distinguished the interior and gave it its focus. The living rooms opened into it. The staircase led to a gallery at first-floor level, off which the bedrooms were situated. This hall, well lighted by its big window on the staircase, made interior corridors unnecessary and provided a sense of size, warmth, and ease which would otherwise have been impossible in a house of modest dimensions.

145 The parsonage, Lanteglos, near Camelford.

146 House, Wilburton, Cambridgeshire.

CHAPTER SEVEN

Princely Buildings and Decorations

After Ackermann published his four slim volumes of designs
in 1835–6 and Pugin had carried out the additions and interior
decorations at Scarisbrick Hall, he could, had he wished to,
have had a lucrative practice as a designer in the decorative
arts and domestic architecture. As he arranged his life and
distributed his talents, he expended the bulk of his energies on
ecclesiastical architecture of one kind and another and did a
great deal of work in the liturgical decorative arts, in church
decoration, and on secular projects.

The metalwork manufactory in which he was partner with
John Hardman assumed major proportions. From a modest
beginning in 1838, it grew until the gross value of the orders
received in 1849 totalled nearly £14,500, of which Pugin
received a percentage, for the designs were his and he acted as
agent for the firm. Much of the inventory consisted of stock
patterns, to which Pugin added annually. He designed articles
specifically for sale to the general public, and he prepared the
drawings for each special order. As the business prospered, he
produced hundreds of new designs each year. All the minutiae
for the Houses of Parliament, including hinges, door plates,
decorative nails, and metal attachments for furniture, candel-
abra, and even umbrella stands and inkwells were specially
drawn in full detail.

Pugin and Hardman were operating a large-scale business
in the mass production of metalwork. Hardman must have
had considerable managerial ability; the drawings show that
Pugin understood the technical aspects of manufacture and the
construction of medieval objects, for he was as insistent about
the 'real thing' in this field as he was in his architecture. Pugin
lived in Ramsgate and produced the drawings there. He was

deeply involved, struggling to get through the work, complaining in letters about the quality and the quantity of their products, or travelling and generating more business. Periodically he would turn up in Birmingham to consult about problems of manufacture or design. But by and large the affairs of the firm were conducted by mail. How well it succeeded may be judged from the comment on the display Pugin and his colleagues presented in the Birmingham Exposition of Arts and Manufactures in 1849; the *Journal of Design* complimented them profusely, mentioning among other things the 'flagon of ruby glass, richly mounted . . . a graceful combination of materials, and a great variety of the processes of manipulation once all-essential in the production of elaborate and artistic metalwork.'

147   Flagon of ruby glass, now in the parish church, Tamworth.

Having become dissatisfied with one glassmaker after another, Pugin convinced Hardman to expand into the manufacture of windows. In the mid-1840s the firm added this second string to its bow: in 1844 Pugin took John Hardman Powell as his apprentice-assistant, and Powell then joined the household in Ramsgate. On occasion other men arrived from Birmingham to live and assist in preparing cartoons for the flood of orders which poured in.

Pugin, who desperately needed privacy, and to whom most others seemed imperfect and singularly deficient in energy, suddenly found himself responsible for a workshop. He still travelled a good deal, but he was at home more and more as his energies were devoted to the design of windows, the preparation of the drawings for the Houses of Parliament, and the supervision of his drawing staff. His irritation increased in direct proportion to his inability to get away from his family and professional household.

The business association with J. G. Crace, which had begun with the building of furniture for the Grange, Ramsgate, was all that Pugin needed to complete his commitment to the decorative side of his practice. Wallpapers, fabrics, furniture, and contracts for whole Pugin interiors were possible when Crace was available to manage the details and manufacture from his designs. George Myers' carving shop continued to make furniture for special settings; among the Myers' papers, there are sheets of Pugin drawings for such items as the rich furniture for Mr Sharples' house in Bishop Eton, Liverpool, which Pugin had designed and was decorating in 1847. Myers was also responsible for the simple but sturdy trestle tables, *prie-dieus*, chests, cabinets, and chairs for the convent in Nottingham, as well as for the carving on the chapel screen.

148   Oswaldcroft, Bishop Eton, Liverpool.

Before 1844 Pugin had done a big business in decorative design. After 1844 it was huge, for he and his staff were supplying an industry in metalwork, glass, furniture, fabrics, wallpapers, sculpture in stone, wall painting, tiles, book bindings, and embroidery. Pugin's achievement is all the more remarkable because he was seriously ill. At the age of thirty-four, he had begun to fear that his life was ending. Only sheer will power and a kind of stubborn optimism enabled him to attend the opening of St Giles'. The Earl of Shrewsbury had himself to make all the arrangements for transporting the choir from St Chad's and for the special railroad transportation and entertainment of the ecclesiastical and lay persons who were his guests on the occasion.

Throughout his life, Pugin accepted occasional work as architect-designer to wealthy gentlemen who wished to embellish their properties, remodel their homes, or build funerary chapels – the latter an enthusiasm particularly suited to Pugin's penchant for Gothic and to his talented improvisations *111–113* upon heraldic material. The Rolle Chapel at Bicton was one of his finest works of this sort; the windows and painting were by Hardman, the tiles by Minton, and the carving and building by Myers. It was Pugin's idea to preserve the fragments of the old church and build the chapel in their midst; Lady Rolle had first wanted an Oriental design.

149 Proof of a woodcut by G. Montbard, 1893, of Alton Towers. The dining-hall window was the last of Pugin's works here. The right wing antedates him.

150 Proof of a wood-cut by G. Montbard, 1893, of Alton Towers, showing the chapel elevation.

About 1837–9, the Earl of Shrewsbury had put Pugin in charge of the works at Alton Towers. Until this decision the architects of the house and garden had been R. Abraham and J. Fradgley, the second of whom, much to his annoyance, was displaced in the Earl's favour by Pugin. In 1837 a part of Alton Towers was described as 'the new suite of apartments which form the western wing'; presumably this is the portion which appears to the right in the view. It was probably Fradgley's last work at the house.

The building of Alton Towers had begun in the 1820s with the construction of the extraordinary long galleries. The new galleries stood apart from the residence, which was, possibly, an older house or a small section of the great living wing planned to follow the completion of the galleries. The conservatory had followed, connecting the residence and galleries. The 'new west apartments', built after the arrival of the sixteenth Earl, had united the far end of the galleries with the house. When Pugin came on the scene, Alton Towers was probably a U-shaped building, bridged by the conservatory. The main entrance was at the base of the block which Pugin changed into the great dining hall in the late 1840s; it was the last of his alterations and additions to the house. The big oriel he added may be seen in the view. The tall tower with its four pinnacles and massive rectangular wing to contain the chapel which Fradgley had built were not finished; Fradgley had begun them, but Pugin was to complete them.

171

It would appear that Pugin had much to do with the external appearance of the chapel as well as its interior decoration, although all of his work involved details rather than the major architectural forms. The structure was certainly there in 1837, for it was described and its dimensions given then. He also repaired the conservatory, furnished and redecorated many of the rooms, and built the tower which bridges the long approach to the entrance of the galleries. (It appears in the foreground in Plate 150.) Even the most cursory examination of the exterior of the chapel and the wings adjacent to it will show that he added bits and pieces, such as second and third storeys, oriels, and doorways all around the chapel and the dining-room block.

Pugin has been given credit and blame for much of Alton Towers with which he had little to do. The house quite upset William Morris, for example, when he passed it on a journey to Staffordshire. If he had looked from the Towers to the hill above the Churnet, he could have seen 'proper' Pugin, which might have pleased him. Pugin seems never to have told the Earl that he should pull his house down and start over again; instead, he patched what was there, added to it when he was asked to, contributed to its decoration, and joined the Earl in such games as the apparelling of the equestrian figure of the Grand Talbot which stood in the big plaster 'chapter house' joining the galleries and the conservatory.

Alton Towers served a certain purpose for Pugin. It is dreadful but also remarkable, and along with his genuine work at Scarisbrick Hall, it brought him fame as a decorator of princely Gothic revival halls. Before a committee of Parliament, Charles Barry cited it as an example of what he hoped the interior of the Houses of Parliament might become. Everyone knew about the Towers, and the Earl's approbation was enough to win Pugin clients. In return for his co-operation on the additions to the Towers, he was given an opportunity to build the beautiful gatehouse at the valley entrance to the estate and the Castle and St John's Hospital on the attractive site opposite.

Other gentlemen sought his services. Lord Midleton asked him to decorate his estates in Surrey and Ireland, and by 1841 Pugin was already at work for him. The programme for the farm buildings, spring house, and lodge at Peper Harow, and for the extensive renovations at Mousehill House nearby, were carefully laid down by Lord Midleton, who was a reader of books on landscape design and architecture and a member of the Cambridge Camden Society. Pugin did his bidding, and mock ruins, which were, of course, stylistically accurate, were the charming result. The Peper Harow barn, the spring, the restorations at Mousehill, and the Norman additions to the parish church are unusual in Pugin's practice, but they are amusing, imaginative, and free of tension because Pugin was doing what Lord Midleton told him to do. Oddly, at the same time Pugin was working at Peper Harow, C. R. Cockerell was employed on additions to the main house – a quite dazzling juxtaposition of personalities.

Mr Henry Drummond, who was as temperamental as Pugin *153–155* and who could be as disagreeable, hired him to add a funerary chapel to the little church of Saints Peter and Paul which stood on the ground of Albury House. There is some confusion about the date of this addition, it being sometimes assigned to the year 1839. Pugin seems, however, never to have visited Albury before 1844, and the work of building the chapel was carried out in 1847.

151 The springhouse, Oxenford Farm, Peper Harow.

The Drummond chantry is one of Pugin's most successful works, for he united his stained glass, tiles, brasses, sculpture, and carving in a whole which was best described by the painter Earley, who was in charge of the 'boys' from Hardman's painting department when the decorations were under way in May 1847. Earley, who seems to have lived in dread of Mr Drummond, whose visits to the chapel were disturbing occasions, had nothing but praise for Pugin's composition. 'It is the most singular design for the walls I ever saw,' he said, 'the arrangement of the patterns making them appear exactly like curtains. The whole chantry appears like some large tent. The pattern is the field of Drummond arms with his crest, a black eagle, displayed thereon.' The screens – one bearing Mr Drummond's apt motto, 'Gang Warily' – and the sculpture and brasses represent Pugin's adroitness in decorative design. His interest in this kind of work must have been more superficial than in Catholic churches and liturgical decorative art, with which he was more deeply involved, but his discipline

152   Sts Peter and Paul, Albury Park.
The Drummond Chapel transept.

153   Sts Peter and Paul, Albury Park.
Interior, the Drummond Chapel.

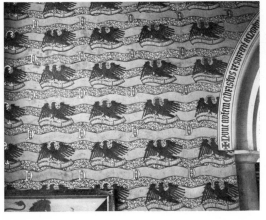

154 The Drummond Chapel, Albury Park. The design is composed of elements of Mr Drummond's arms.

155 The screen, Drummond Chapel, Albury.

was so great that he could extemporize with facility, a talent he exploited in the thousands of drawings he was preparing for the Houses of Parliament.

The brick exterior of Albury House, often attributed to Pugin but doubtfully so, would have been a late work if indeed it was his at all. A galvanized iron veranda for the main front, which was in place as late as 1872 but no longer is, was ordered from John Hardman in 1848. An 1849 drawing for the same front, in the collections of the Royal Institute of British Architects, illustrates a much more sensitive treatment of the new surface of the house than it ultimately received. The drawing, covered with many corrections in a hand other than Pugin's, suggests that work was only beginning in 1849 and that Mr Drummond was considering what he would and would not accept of Pugin's proposal. It seems entirely possible that Edward Welby Pugin planned the garden and other elevations after 1852, just as he carried on others of his father's tasks at Alton Towers, Chirk Castle, Burton Close, Ushaw College, the cathedral in Shrewsbury, the convents at Birr and Water-ford, the Irish cathedrals, and West Tofts.

156   The Pugin addition (central portion), Bilton Grange, Rugby.

Bilton Grange, Rugby, is Pugin's least successful venture. Captain Hibbert was his most difficult client; he quarrelled with Pugin and Myers, badgered them incessantly, complained without cause, and altered plans in the course of building. Furthermore, he refused to spend the money required to obtain the baronial effect he sought and was finally annoyed when his house did not turn out well. Despite these difficulties Pugin managed to make the dining hall presentable, and the suite of two large rooms that he built conveys a feeling of conviction and some style. The kitchen must once have been one of his better efforts. Bilton Grange is marred by an ugly entrance hall, a useless and pretentious gallery that seems to have been inspired by the gargantuan and graceless Fradgley galleries at Alton Towers, and by the fact that the house was ultimately a clumsy mixture of a pair of earlier houses, one of which was Georgian, and the Hibbert-Pugin addition, which accorded in no way with the original buildings to which it was attached.

Because of its size and the fact that its design may be related *160 – 162* to Pugin's proposal of 1841 for Garendon House, Maynooth College, near Dublin, belongs among his princely works. The college is severe, massive, barren and commanding, but it lacks *130, 163* the grace of Ratcliffe College and the beauty of Pugin's Irish

157 Bilton Grange, near Rugby. That portion of the house carrying Captain Hibbert's initials in the brickwork, the four major bays and the balustrade.

158 The kitchen wing and chimney, Bilton Grange, Rugby.

159 The balustrade, Bilton Grange, Rugby.

parish churches. Maynooth has all the stoniness of his Irish cathedrals, but it has neither the variety of forms nor the height which provided their drama.

Dreamed-of mansions were sometimes destined to remain no more than dreams. The Garendon scheme, to which reference has been made in connection with Pugin's churches, lives on only in drawings. The equally fanciful proposal for a huge manor house near Stroud for William Leigh was also never carried out. Mr Leigh seems to have desired to establish a medieval community that would include not only his

88

177

160 Ink drawing by Pugin, 1841. Proposed design for the rebuilding of Garendon House.

161 Maynooth College, main entrance to the quadrangle.

162 Maynooth College, the quadrangle; the towers illustrated in Plate 161 lie behind the rectangular feature on the left.

demesne but the neighbouring villages. Like the Garendon proposal, the imaginative, stately and elegantly Gothic house that Pugin conceived survives only as a book of pretty pen and ink drawings. Mr Leigh was not a man easily defeated by the forces of reality, however, and years later he embarked upon – but never completed – a huge stone mansion with Benjamin Bucknell as his architect. About the ruin of their unfinished building the shadow of Pugin lingers. Its general plan and appearance, and especially the design of the chapel, resemble the house Pugin had suggested; Mr Leigh was inclined to hand over drawings Pugin had prepared to other architects who promised to build from them for less than Pugin's estimates.

Mr Leigh had also approached Pugin about a church and monastery he hoped to build at Stroud on the edge of his estate; again Pugin discovered there was not enough money to carry out the work satisfactorily. In 1846, when he was ill and deeply concerned about the future of his practice, Pugin knew that another architect would undertake Mr Leigh's task. Charles Hansom was waiting; the church at Stroud, like those at Hanley Swan, Erdington, Rugeley, and the convents at Clifton and Stapehill, are by Hansom in Pugin's manner.

If he could not build churches, Pugin could have the satisfaction of furnishing those built by others. The names of architects began to appear among the clients of the metalwork and stained glass businesses; they included William Butterfield, R. C. Carpenter – the chosen designer of the Ecclesiological Society – A. Salvin, Fuljames and Waller, the Hansoms, Penson of Oswestry, Scoles, Matthew Hadfield, S. Daukes, and, of course, Charles Barry. Hansom's churches in Hanley Swan and Erdington each possess a full display of Pugin fittings and metalwork of every kind.

163 Ink drawing by Pugin, 1841. Proposed design for Garendon House.

The scale, quality, and coherence of Pugin's contribution to the decoration of the Houses of Parliament should be emphasized. The massive task of designing and holding the project together through the complex history of the construction of the building belonged to Charles Barry, who saw its potential and made it reality. Even if he had no other fine buildings to his credit, the Houses of Parliament would have been enough to guarantee him a place at the head of his profession. But Barry was completely occupied with the building problems, and it is only fair to observe that he could not have done the decorations even if he had had the time to prepare them. His sketch-books show that he had a firm grasp of Gothic architecture; they do not demonstrate Pugin's almost intuitive mastery of the style. Pugin could think in Gothic and Barry could not. The decorations are definitely Pugin's, and they are the largest of his works on a princely scale.

Charles Barry was particular about each part of the decoration's being brought to perfection; no one but he could tell how the details fitted together. Barry was responsible for the many revisions of the gates for the House of Lords, and it was he who returned the gas chandeliers for the Peers Library to Hardman for a correction in the design – two examples of the many which show his precise and demanding leadership. It is significant that there are almost no letters from Barry complaining about the style or execution of any of the objects supplied by Pugin, although he did protest when Hardman was slow in delivering what he had ordered. It would appear that the work produced from Pugin's drawings was, by and large, entirely satisfactory.

Pugin did not simply do what he was told. In consultation with Barry – conferences which frequently took place at the site of the building operations in London – he came to understand the function and specifications for an object or fitment, then proceeded to produce detailed drawings of them in suitable style, with manufacturing instructions as well. The creative act was Pugin's, for it was he who united technical and stylistic

164   Interior of the
House of Lords.

165   The throne,
House of Lords.

knowledge and devised the ingenious adaptations of late medieval ornamental detail to nineteenth-century use. More often than not he worked without a medieval model because there was none. Medieval candlesticks, chalices, jewellery, stained glass, and furniture could be copied, although Pugin rarely did so, but umbrella stands, inkwells, clocks, calendars, gas chandeliers, and wallpapers required an inventive genius which Pugin possessed but carefully restrained in his religious works out of respect for tradition.

Pugin's second contribution was the homogeneity he alone could supply from his knowledge of medieval art and ornament, his comprehension of technical processes in metal fabrication, carving, painted decoration, glass and papers, his sensitivity to the history and principles of design, and his ability to maintain consistency and control over every inch of the interior. All the details were interrelated; the interior of the House of Lords is remarkable in many ways, most importantly in the strong impression it gives of being the work of a single artist. Pugin's hand is everywhere apparent.

Barry's presence can be felt in this cohesive and unique interior, for like an impresario he saw to it that Pugin's stellar performance was perfectly recorded, that nothing qualified its impact and totality. The Houses of Parliament would not have been successful had it not been for the commanding imagination and taste of Charles Barry, who recognized and understood the nature of Pugin's gift, nurtured its power, and provided an opportunity for its expression.

The Houses of Parliament is one of the great buildings of the nineteenth century. It was conceived as a work to be built in a single intense programme within a limited time, and it was intended to serve a specific purpose – to house a modern parliamentary government – and to celebrate in its design the history of the nation and the institution. A collaboration was required because the work was so large and complex and the time in which to execute it so short. The Houses therefore prefigure the complex questions of design attribution which were to arise in modern architecture as groups of architects, engineers, and technical specialists joined their skills to produce single buildings.

Whatever their work together had been in 1835–6, this last phase of the Barry-Pugin partnership was a true collaboration. And it was one that Pugin never resented. Out of it came the finest interiors the Gothic revival was ever to produce; although they were in no sense truly Gothic, they were a resolved statement of Victorian preferences. Pugin produced one design after another – he said he prepared two thousand for the House of Lords alone – from his store of memories and from his admiration for and knowledge of medieval art, but the importance of his contribution depends as solidly on his sound understanding of contemporary methods of manufacture. To Charles Barry the building owes its clarity of plan and its efficiency, the seclusion of its interior from the disturbances of the outside world, the spaciousness of its rooms, and the dramatic quality given them by their delicate detail.

The initiation of the decoration of the Houses of Parliament gave Pugin's fame a new impetus. To satisfy the clients it brought him, he solidified his association with J. G. Crace into a business. Pugin needed money to build his church at Ramsgate. He could turn out decorations by the roomful, for he could utilize the metalwork patterns on file with Hardman, the sculptors in Myers' shop, the tile patterns in the possession of Minton, and the furniture, wallpapers and fabrics Crace had manufactured from his designs. The result of this late blossoming of Pugin's practice is a cluster of contracts for decoration in what can be termed his 'Houses of Parliament' style. Crace supervised the installations, and Pugin rarely if ever visited the houses before, during, or after they were completed. The interiors at Eastnor and Lismore Castles and those at Leighton *166, 167* Hall belong in this category. So routine had this work become by the time of Pugin's death that his associates went on producing houses of his kind, such as Abney and Horsted, after he was gone.

In a sense it was sad that the Houses of Parliament and the mansions and castles of rich men that Pugin decorated in his last years should have been reversions to and celebrations of one of his earliest accomplishments, the delicate and imaginative illustrations of the interiors of the Deanery of 1833. He is too often remembered for his extravagance rather than for the simplicity, subtlety, and restraint of so much of his work in the decorative arts; the elaborate objects have found their way into museums or have been photographed and discussed in print, whereas the simpler things have gone quietly on serving their owners, their identity as Pugin's works unregarded or forgotten. The Medieval Court at the Great Exhibition was the last public appearance of Pugin and his fabricators. His perfectionism and taste still dominated their display but some of the fire had gone out of it. The technically complex and excessively ornamented object predominated, and unlike their contribution to the earlier Birmingham exhibition, this one contained little that was new or fresh. The man who had provided the special energy was failing, and the group was beginning to fall apart. Myers had begun to look for jobs elsewhere; Hardman and Crace had begun to panic as they felt their businesses threatened. Pugin was ill, petulant, depressed, sometimes irrational in his anger and despair, and involved beyond his depth in religious controversy.

166   Entrance hall, Leighton Hall, Welshpool.

CHAPTER EIGHT

The Last Years

More, perhaps, than his failing health and the change in his practice, two events of the years 1846–8 shattered the image Pugin had of himself and made him question the value of his accomplishments. From the beginning of his career he had been haunted by the knowledge that his best efforts sank 'when tested by the scale of antient excellence'. In the year 1846, there were some who were ready to assure him that his worst fears were justified. His churches, many of them built in his first years of practice, were available to anyone for analysis and discovery of failings. In 1848, others began to express doubts that Pugin's religious and social missions had been of value to his faith. His campaigns and feelings had been so intense and high-pitched that he could not gracefully retreat from the positions he had taken on Catholic ecclesiastical art. To change his mind or recant his opinions would have been an admission of defeat and a desertion of his ideas and ideals. Yet he was defeated, for he had lost his audience.

The attack on Pugin in the *Ecclesiologist* in the year 1846 was an astute and calculated act of cruelty. It raised all the doubts applicable to any serious and devout Gothic revival designer, implying, however, that they were relevant to Pugin alone. When the author said, 'It is now rather time to warn our readers that Mr Pugin's churches are not literal revivals of medieval churches, but rather conventional and modernized reflections of them', he could as easily have substituted the name of either R. C. Carpenter or William Butterfield, of whom the Ecclesiological Society heartily approved, or of any number of other architects who were participating in the revival. The author reproved Pugin for having been 'taken up' by *Punch*; but he did not say how Pugin might have avoided it, nor did he

◀ 167   The suite of rooms on the north front, Leighton Hall, Welshpool. The doors, fireplaces, ceiling decoration all by Pugin and Crace.

recognize that the jokes were prompted by his work at the Houses of Parliament. With solemnity and crocodile tears, the author admitted that Pugin had been the first to enter the lists in defence of Gothic.

We are in our measure (we mean this reservation most sincerely) responsible for the reputation of Christian art; and persons might confound the capacities of true art with Mr Pugin's mannerisms. This pressing danger now makes us come forward, else we should much rather have been silent. We have, we repeat it, a great respect for Mr Pugin, and we feel great gratitude to him for what we have learned; and much we have learned, we are glad to be able to acknowledge it, from him; but still we have no other course than this open to us; and most truly happy shall we be if our observations should falsify themselves by making Mr Pugin not what he has shown himself in his latter works, but what once we thought of him, what modest industry can make him.

In January 1846, S.N. Stokes and F.A. Paley resigned all connection with the *Ecclesiologist* and the Ecclesiological Society and protested this attack, which they called 'puerile' and 'ungenerous'. Both gentlemen then became converts to Catholicism. Pugin chose to answer the *Ecclesiologist* in a letter to *The Tablet*. There was no way to respond, save to apologize for the error of his ways. Although he was angry, Pugin did just that, saying that St Giles', Cheadle, would prove his critics were wrong and that lack of money for his buildings had been the cause of his mistakes. The unrealistic standards by which he had been judged were his own as well, and he had begun to lose his nerve.

The *Ecclesiologist* had done its work well, for it dwelt on the most vulnerable aspects of Pugin's work. St Chad's took a drubbing; St Barnabas' was condemned with faint praise and criticized for the very qualities which make it most interesting; St Oswald's and Pugin's other churches were not mentioned. Apparently to the particular delight of the author, Pugin's illustrations of his buildings provided certain illogicalities for remark and attack. The article was correct in saying that Pugin

186

had split upon the rocks of 'quickness and versatility', yet it was these very qualities which also made him one of the greatest designers and most exciting theorists of his generation.

In July 1848, the *Rambler*, a new Catholic journal, was founded by J. M. Capes, with the approval of John Henry Newman and Bishop Wiseman. Capes intended his paper to reach the 'old Catholics' whom Pugin had been attempting to educate; he hoped the *Rambler* would raise the standard of both clerical and lay education and promote discussion of social issues without political bias. Only six months after the new journal began publication, the subject of Catholic art and architecture, and particularly the troublesome question of rood-screens, cropped up in its columns. Joseph L. Altholz, in his book on Capes and his policies, summarizes the conclusions that emerged from this discussion: 'It was more important, the *Rambler* asserted, to build many small cheap churches among the poor than a few grandiose Gothic edifices; it was better to spend little on decoration and much on schools; and it was preferable to sacrifice the austere beauties of plain-chant in favour of popular hymns in English, such as Faber was writing.' It is impossible to ignore the validity of these arguments, for the *Rambler* was genuinely concerned about vital issues; its position was not one of self-seeking and selfish aggrandizement, as had been the case with the *Ecclesiologist*.

Pugin's answer was contained in his pamphlet *Some Remarks on the Articles Which Have Recently Appeared in the 'Rambler'*, of 1850, and in his book *A Treatise on Chancel Screens and Rood Lofts*, of 1851. To understand Pugin and his collapse one must read both, for although he was writing in anger, he was withdrawing from position after position he had taken in his writing and in his practice. He disowned his own works: St Giles' had been painted because of an afterthought of its noble founder; St George's 'was spoilt by the very instructions laid down by the committee. . . . In consequence height, proportion, everything, was sacrificed to meet these conditions'; in his comments

S. Augustins. Ramsgate

168 Ink drawing, by Pugin, 1848. The Grange and St Augustine's, Ramsgate,
certain features of which were never built. Pugin's tomb is in the chantry.

on St Barnabas', he repeated what the *Ecclesiologist* had published four years earlier. None of his remarks agreed with what he had said about the buildings when he built them. The disappointment of an 'antient agitator' is contained in his statement, 'I have passed my life in thinking of fine things, studying fine things, designing fine things, and realizing very poor ones'. Only a decade had gone by since the day in 1841 when, filled with high hopes and conviction in the righteousness and virtues of his ideas and artistic insights, he had declared that he would 'revive not invent'.

In the autumn and winter of 1851 Pugin was seriously ill and frightened and depressed over his physical condition and the damage his incapacity was doing to his practice. His family responsibilities were heavy. Four years of loneliness had followed the death of his second wife, Louisa, in 1844; Pugin had managed his household of six children, with the assistance of governesses and servants. He had sought to remarry in these years but had twice been rejected by ladies to whom he proposed. In 1848 he married for a third time. Jane Knill Pugin brought stability into his personal affairs, and she promptly presented him with two more children, Margaret, born in 1849 and Peter Paul, born in 1851. Jane Pugin supported her husband in all his views, assisted him in his last and frightening illness, and did all she could to keep his reputation alive after his death.

In January and February 1852, Pugin's physical condition deteriorated. He was in constant pain, and he complained that he was suffering from a return of a kidney ailment. He had never been able to tolerate inactivity, and now he was cut off from his work. 'The drowsiness still continues', he wrote. 'I have been obliged to sleep four times today. . . . My head becomes heavy, my hand shakes and I am obliged to stop.' Late in February while on a business trip to London Pugin became violent and confused, and his colleagues John Hardman, Crace, Myers, and his personal friend the painter J. R. Herbert advised Mrs Pugin to commit her husband to a private mental hospital in the outskirts of London. When he showed no signs of improvement he was placed in Bethlehem Hospital in June 1852, where the physician in charge of his case diagnosed his illness as 'mania'.

When the public became aware that Pugin had been placed in Bethlehem there was a general outcry that a man so distinguished and remarkable should receive shabby treatment and become a public charge. In September 1852, Mrs Pugin removed her husband from Bethlehem, hired male nurses and attempted to care for him in a house she had rented in Hammersmith. Pugin improved somewhat under the care of doctors who sedated him with chloroform. After several weeks, and at Pugin's request, she took him home to Ramsgate, where for a few hours he seemed aware of his surroundings, happy to be back among his books and drawings, but he refused to rest. On his third day at home Pugin died as the result of a seizure which seems to have been a stroke. He was buried in his church of 168 St Augustine, in the Pugin chantry.

Conclusion

Pugin set out to practise architecture and to change it. He succeeded in both, but when he asked himself late in his life what he had accomplished he was not happy with the answer. It is now possible to understand the nature of his contribution and to appraise its significance as he could not.

The quality which set Pugin apart from other writers and architects of his generation was best defined by a reviewer who in 1844 asked himself why and how Pugin was unusual. After having roundly condemned Charles Barry for his willingness to work in any number of styles 'like a universal genius', he turned to Pugin and said that he was 'almost the only architect in England who has seen the absurdity of this cosmopolite practice'. Pugin was to be praised, said the author, for his earnest pursuit of his chosen style. 'In these copying days . . . it is something to have an architect who has so thoroughly studied the style in which he is to build that he can copy it correctly, and his buildings have not only the general form but really the meaning and some of the spirit of the ancient ones.' When Pugin enlarged his concept of style to include its 'meaning' and 'spirit', he had added a new dimension to the use of history and historical data in architecture. He had assigned eclecticism a new responsibility, and in so doing he had been forced to reconsider the nature of every building detail, of every structural practice, and of the relationship that should prevail between the design and function of a building, and between architecture and the society of which it was an expression. As other architects did not, he saw buildings as projections of the way of life in which they were produced, and he considered the whole building and its role rather than the vagaries of style.

Studies of architectural theory and the history of Gothic art

191

and architecture were established disciplines in Pugin's lifetime. Men such as Alfred Bartholomew – whose *Specifications for Practical Architecture* appeared in 1841 – Robert Willis, William Whewell, James Fergusson, and G. R. Lewis, as well as members of the ecclesiological movement, archaeologists and topographers, and innumerable informed amateurs, were publishing books. Some, such as the works of Bartholomew, Whewell, Willis, and Fergusson, were brilliant; others were useful studies of particular buildings and places. The proposals of the ecclesiologists and their cohorts and of other Protestant churchmen were well informed but doctrinaire. Foreign books were also influential in England, and at least one of Pugin's principles may have been inspired by the works of George Moller, a German authority on medieval architecture. There were, as well, important earlier writers to be considered, among whom were Thomas Hope and Thomas Rickman. Even a cursory review of the journals for the years 1835–51 reveals that a highly intelligent running discussion on architecture and books about it was being carried on in periodicals like the *Quarterly Review* and *Westminster Review*, as well as in those devoted to the arts and architecture. It was in this company that Pugin's writing appeared and found its place.

Almost every point in Pugin's books may have found fuller expression in one or another of the works that have been mentioned. A man as knowledgeable as Pugin would surely have known the writing of Robert Willis; certainly the statements on verticality in *True Principles* resemble those of Whewell. But Pugin cannot be explained away as an author of pastiche. His observations may have been similar to those of others, but the uses to which he put them and the order he gave them quite altered and reconstituted them. It was one thing for Moller to note that in Gothic architecture decoration was a product of construction and another for Pugin to amplify this observation by saying that as a generalization it was true of all fine architecture. Pugin certainly knew Jacques-François Blondel's comment that style was an expression of the reasons for and nature of a building and that Gothic conveyed religious meaning, but the application of these ideas in the nineteenth century was far from Blondel's intent. Again, it was Pugin's concern for the whole building, for the unification of style, purpose, structure, and decoration – and his belief that distortion of their proper relationship was somehow more than an artistic error – which constituted his contribution to architectural thinking.

Pugin was unique in other ways. He was a man of literary talent as well as a prolific and original practising architect and artist. His books acquired an added dimension because he was a designer; his buildings were sought out and studied because he had written so well about them and had stated his theory of design in clear and appealing terms. The wit of his caricatures and the convincing illustrations of his own and medieval buildings clarified and demonstrated his arguments. He was no academic; his scholarship was directed to practical purposes, to the solution of specific design problems, to the discovery of medieval models, and to the unearthing of historical precedents to justify their use. After he had completed the second volume of *Examples of Gothic Architecture*, all of his books were directed to the lay public – particularly to the Catholic public – and the architectural community. He never published a treatise on a medieval building, as other architects did in the course of their careers.

Finally, Pugin was an architect, and to that title he would surely have prefixed the word Catholic. His creativity kept him searching; he brought news of the Nazarene school to England; he experimented with working arrangements with craftsmen and builders and devised methods of manufacture from his designs that he hoped would transform them into objects readily and inexpensively available; he kept himself informed of restoration work in progress on the Continent; he made himself an authority on medieval art and became a notable collector of books and prints. Fame came his way and yet he did not allow himself to stagnate. He could have satisfied his clientele with many versions of his early churches, but instead he progressed brilliantly until the compositional suggestions in his last buildings became the basis for the generation of churches that would follow his.

The Gothic revival had begun long before Pugin's time, but he was able to hasten its ascendancy and increase its influence. His artistic, intellectual, and literary bearing secured attention for the causes he championed. His intransigent dedication to his faith and art and the tragic denouement of his life endowed the ideas for which he fought with an uncommon authority.

Sadly enough, Pugin was too close to see what he had accomplished or even, perhaps, to understand the implications of his ideas and work. In 1851, looking back in sorrow, he wrote to John Hardman:

My writings, much more than what I have been able to do, have revolutionized the taste of England. My cause as an architect is run out. I always told you when the tide begins it must run out. I am really ashamed of our things. I feel perfectly miserable. I never felt such despondency of drawing fine things. You know in your heart it is true. Our things are only good when compared with the Beasts, the Brutes who belong to this age, but by the true standard they make me ill. As we gain knowledge conviction of failure is inevitable. It quite gets on my mind. I believe we know too much. Knowledge is power but it is misery. Dear me, a few years ago I felt quite satisfied with things we now look upon as abominable. Still I almost sigh for old simplicity when I thought all the old cathedral men fine fellows. It is all delusion. Everything is deception and unreal vanity and vexation of spirit. I shall turn an anchorite at last, with a companion. A new order, a development of hermit.

Buildings and some other works

The list that follows is not complete, for it does not include all Pugin's stained glass windows, or much of his metalwork, wallpapers, vestments, and jewellery still being used by churches or individuals or now in the possession of museums. It does, however, include all his major architecture and the larger projects for which he made design proposals that were never carried out, and it also locates the notable collections of his ecclesiastical metalwork – Erdington Abbey, a Charles Hansom building, appears here, for example, because of the Pugin fittings and decorations in which it is so rich. When an extensive comment on a building is included in the text of the book its entry in this list is short.

I have studied most of Pugin's buildings at first hand, but because of their number I have not yet had an opportunity to check on some works, the existence of which has been suggested by a surviving drawing or drawings. A few examples of this kind are included here because the drawing or drawings were of sufficient merit to warrant notice.

The listing is arranged by two-year periods, and within each of these alphabetically by place name. Specific dates appear within each entry.

1827–1835

In an autobiographical account, written about 1831–2, Pugin stated that in February 1827, he had begun 'furniture for Carlton Palace for Morel, previous to their removal to Windsor Castle' and that on 26 June he 'went to design and make working drawings of Gothic furniture for Windsor Castle'. He specified that he designed the furniture for 'the long gallery, coffee rooms, vestibule, ante-room, great staircase, Octagon room in the Brunswick Tower, great dining room' and that he supervised the work at Seddons, Aldersgate Street. He implied, though he did not state, that he designed the cast-iron chandeliers for the gallery that he said were made by Summers of Bond Street.

In the same report of his activities Pugin said he first met James Gillespie Graham in 1829–31 (he is not precise about the date nor does he describe the circumstances) and that at Graham's order he designed the interiors of a 'large mansion', work consisting of 'the great hall, Chapel, entrance hall, staircase, ante-room, library, drawing room', all of which were 'James I' except the drawing room which was 'Louis XIV'.

After working as a stage carpenter at Covent Garden in November 1830, Pugin began a business of his own in carving and joining, with furniture as his speciality. His shop was the upper loft, 12 Hart Street, Covent Garden. A number of pen and ink drawings, dated 1831 (Royal

Institute of British Architects and the Victoria and Albert Museum), substantiate his statement; they are all of furniture and metal fittings.

Benjamin Ferrey, who knew Pugin well, said in his Pugin biography that this first venture into business failed shortly after it began. This disappointment may have prompted Pugin to return to the theatre, and in March 1831, he built two scenes for the ballet *Kenilworth*; the backcloths of each were by W. Grieve. On the recommendation of Grieve Pugin was then employed to build a temporary private theatre and stage for the Marquis of Stafford. Some studies for stage settings by Pugin are in the Royal Institute of British Architects.

The death of his young wife and his father in 1832, followed by those of his mother and Miss Selina Welby, his aunt, left Pugin with a modest inheritance consisting of his father's publications – which were still in demand – and his aunt's financial assets. The years 1832–5 were a time of training and decision. In that period, Pugin resolved to turn his talents to architecture. He became a Catholic, and he re-established his family when he married for a second time. He travelled in England and abroad, sketching and exercising his talents as a critic and draughtsman.

Pugin settled in Salisbury where he found sympathetic friends with whom he had worked in the restoration of the medieval house of John Halle in 1834. His architectural career began there in 1835.

1835–1836

Alderbury, Wiltshire. St Marie's Grange. 1835.

Drawings for decorative details and furniture, the King Edward VI Grammar School, Birmingham.

Assistance in the preparation of the competition drawings, the Houses of Parliament.

1836

Further work on the Houses of Parliament, autumn.

(FOR CHARLES BARRY)

1835

Drawings for a church.
Drawings for a house.
Competition drawings, the Houses of Parliament.

1836

A series of drawings, unspecified as to kind or place, August 1836.

A set of twenty-six drawings prepared in September 1836. They were followed by thirty-two further drawings, September–October 1836.

    6 north door
  22 west end
   5 interior west end
   1 large west front.

(FOR JAMES GILLESPIE GRAHAM)

Drawings for Mr H (possibly Hull, Wardour Street, furniture manufacturer).

Drawings, unidentified, for Colonel Baker.

1837–1838

Alton, Staffordshire. Alton Towers. Began supervision of the works there in September 1837. Continued as the architect to the Earl of Shrewsbury until 1852.

Alderbury, Wiltshire. Clarendon Park. A gatehouse. 1837.

Derby. St Mary's, December 1837–October 1839.

Dudley, Worcestershire. Our Lady and St Thomas of Canterbury. Begun, October 1838, with a drawing for the exterior from the east and one of the interior, both for a much more elaborate church than was ultimately built. Further drawings, presumably those used, June 1839. Presbytery is also by Pugin. A porch has been added to the west front of this church. (See note on Dewsbury, Additional Information.)

Keighley, Yorkshire. St Anne's. Drawings May 1838. (The church has been much altered.)

London. Bermondsey. The Convent of Mercy. 1838. (Now largely destroyed.)

Macclesfield, Cheshire. St Alban's. Drawings December 1838. Foundation stone April 1839. Opened 1841.

Manchester. Designs for an elaborate church for Manchester which was never built. Drawings have survived. October 1838.

Newport, Shropshire. Additions and repairs to the parish church. At the order of the Earl of Shrewsbury, 1838.

Ormskirk, Lancashire. Scarisbrick Hall. Pugin began to work at Scarisbrick in April 1837, and continued into the mid-1840s. Many changes and additions by E. W. Pugin.

Reading, Berkshire. St James'. Foundation stone, December 1837. (Much altered.)

Solihull, Warwickshire. St Augustine's. Begun April 1838. Porch and chancel by C. Hansom.

Southport, Lancashire. St Marie's. Opened 1840. (Much altered.)

Sutton Coldfield, Warwickshire. Completion of the buildings at Oscott College. The Chapel 1837–8. Drawings for metalwork.

Uttoxeter, Staffordshire. St Mary's. Opened August 1839. Presbytery by Pugin. (Church much altered.)

Wexford, Eire. Chapel, St Peter's College. Foundation stone June 1838.

Whitby, Yorkshire. Designs for St Hilda's. 1838. (Now replaced by another building.)

1837

Drawings for Holyrood Chapel.
Drawings for a church.

1838

A number of drawings, unspecified place or purpose.

(FOR JAMES GILLESPIE GRAHAM)

1837

Drawings for a chapel.
Assistance Houses of Parliament designs, 1837, spring.

(FOR CHARLES BARRY)

A design for a chalice and a ciborium for the Birmingham Catholic chapel. 1837.

Metal-work designs for the Reverend Dr Rock, Chaplain to the Earl of Shrewsbury. 1837.

Benjamin Ferrey said that Pugin prepared designs for Longford Castle. Work proposed was never executed.

Drawings for the Reverend Dr Doyle, St George's, Southwark. Metalwork. 1838.

Buildings attributed to Pugin,
198

1837–1838 but attribution not confirmed.

Parish churches at Ramsgrange and Bree, Wexford, Eire.

1839–1840

Alton, Staffordshire. St John's Hospital (now St John the Baptist and the Convent of the Sisters of Mercy). Presbytery and house adjacent to it built or extensively rebuilt by Pugin. Drawings for the Hospital, September 1839. Building begun 1840. The school attached to the Convent is not that illustrated in the *Present States* and is probably not by A. W. Pugin. E. W. Pugin was working at Alton in 1854.

Banbury, Oxfordshire. Various drawings for St John's were made in 1839. Further drawings 1840–2. School and presbytery and additions to the church, including the chancel, are by Pugin. The church is by Derick, the presbytery has been faced with stone, the school replaced.

Birmingham. Metropolitan Cathedral Church of St Chad. Contract drawings 1839.
Convent of Mercy, Handsworth. Drawings 1840.
Bishop's House, Birmingham. Drawings 1840–1.

Cambridge. St Andrew's. Drawings 1840. Estimates 1841, 1842 charges for furnishing. Wailes glass. Opened 1843. (Demolished or moved.)

Cheadle, Staffordshire. St Giles'. Drawings for the church completed December 1840. Subsequent revisions in the design 1841–4. Opened 1846. The school, convent and presbytery are also by Pugin.

Gorey, Wexford, Eire. St Michael, the Archangel. 1839. The convent is by Pugin but is later than the church.

Liverpool. St Oswald's. Drawings completed late 1840. (Church now replaced by another.)

London. St George's, Southwark. Proposal 1839. Second design autumn 1840. Opened 1848. (Destroyed in the Second World War.)

Manchester. St Wilfrid's, Hulme. Design 1839.

Mount St Bernard's Abbey, Leicestershire. Design 1840.

Newport, Shropshire. Additional designs for the parish church.

Oxford. Design for a church in Oxford, never built. 1840.

Radford, Oxfordshire. Holy Trinity. Designed 1839. Opened 1841.

Rathfarnham, Dublin. Design proposal for the Chapel, Loreto Abbey. Drawings 1839.

Stratton-on-the-Fosse, Somerset. Designs for Downside Abbey. 1839. Never built.

Ushaw College, Durham. Proposal for a large chapel and college buildings. 1840. Chapel completed 1848, but not to the 1840 design. College buildings still in progress in 1852. Since rebuilt.

Warwick Bridge, Cumberland. Our Lady and St Wilfrid. Drawings for the church and presbytery 1840.

A number of orders for designs from James Gillespie Graham and Charles Barry.

Pugin also continued to supervise building activity at and design for Oscott College; Scarisbrick Hall; Alton and Alton Towers; the churches at Derby, Dudley, Macclesfield, Wexford, and Gorey; and to prepare designs for metalwork, laces, sculpture and stained glass.

1841–1842

Beaufort Castle, Inverness. Drawings prepared for Lord Lovat 1842. Pugin described them as plans for the restoration of 'the old Priory' and the building of two houses.

Beverley, Yorkshire. St Mary's. First negotiations over the work of restoration of St Mary's, 1842. Pugin was still at work there at the time of his death in 1852. E. W. Pugin continued in the 1850s. A. W. Pugin's work at St Mary's was more extensive than has hitherto been realized; he designed doors, parapets; dealt with drainage problems in the church and crypt; laid new flooring; provided new seating, decoration and West window, 1850. Bilton Grange, Rugby, Warwickshire. Pugin started work at Bilton Grange in 1841 and continued until 1851. First plans were fairly modest; extensive addition to the two older houses composing the Grange made 1846–7. Two gatehouses on the estate are probably from Pugin designs.

Brewood, Staffordshire. St Mary's. Begun 1842. Built 1843–4. Opened 1844. Presbytery and school buildings also by Pugin. Grave monument and brass to the Reverend Robert Richmond, Pugin 1850. Glass by Wailes to Pugin design. Earl of Shrewsbury contributed to cost of building.

Edinburgh. St Mary's Cathedral. In 1841 *The Catholic Magazine* reported that St Mary's had been reopened after a complete remodelling of its interior. The work was said to have been carried out by Mr Gillespie Graham; it included enlargement of the sanctuary, addition of an oak screen, the latter carved 'in the richest manner' and based on 'the best models of the Gothic of the Middle Ages'. The new pulpit was described as being in 'the light and florid Gothic style'.

In 1840–1 Pugin was paid £200 by Graham for unspecified work.

Garendon and Grace Dieu Houses, Leicestershire. Drawings for the re-

building of Garendon House, 1841. Drawings for additions and repairs to the chapel at Grace Dieu House – screen, benches, two canopies, triptych, font, pulpit, sepulchre, sedilia, pair of altar candlesticks – and the building of the gate to the service courtyard of the house. A second set of drawings for the Grace Dieu chapel is dated 1848; they include the new screen, the ciborium, tracery and the belfry.

Kenilworth, Warwickshire. St Augustine's. Church and presbytery by Pugin. Church 1841–2 and enlarged 1842–52.

Killarney, Eire. St Mary's. Ground laid out and first drawings prepared 1842. E. W. Pugin designed the altar in 1854. Building not completed until the twentieth century.

Kirkham, Lancashire. St John the Evangelist. Begun 1842. Pugin's drawings for the organ gallery and the pulpit are dated 1844. Large orders for metalwork and a brass Communion rail, 1845. (Much altered interior.)

Leadenham, Lincolnshire. St Swithin's. Decoration of the chancel roof. 1841.

Leeds. Cathedral Church of St Anne. Altar, reredos and screen ordered by the Reverend Father Walmsley at the request of the donor, Miss Grace Humble of Birtley and Leeds. Only the altar and reredos survive. This work, which cost upwards of

£600, is one of Pugin's finest of its kind. Design 1842.

Liverpool. Convent of the Sisters of Mercy. Two periods of building represented at the convent, the first 1841–2, and the second 1847. (The community has now moved from the building, which in 1969 was scheduled for demoliton.)

St Marie's. 1841–2. (Now demolished.)

London, Chelsea. Designs for St Mary's, Cadogan Street. Plans for a 'hospital', in fact a school and almshouses, for Mr Knight. Pugin's drawing of the ground plan is extant. The school was built in 1841–2; the almshouses, which have been greatly rebuilt and repaired, are still in use. Fragments of the school building survive.

Woolwich. St Peter's. Begun spring 1842, final decorations still being ordered in 1850. East end altered, tower and spire never completed. The smaller presbytery next to the church is by Pugin; his drawings for it survive.

Manchester. Plans never used for St John's, Salford. 1842.

Neston, Cheshire. St Winifride's. Attributed to Pugin. Although the church is unlike any other by Pugin the house and school do resemble his work. There were numerous metal-work orders for this church placed by the Reverend R. Gillow, 1841. Opened 1843.

Newcastle-upon-Tyne. Cathedral Church of St Mary. Begun 1841 and completed, except for the tower and spire, in 1844. Pulpit, font, altars, screens were from Pugin designs. Position of the tower is as Pugin planned it, but the design is not his but C. Hansom's.

Nottingham. Cathedral Church of St Barnabas and the Bishop's House. Begun 1841 and completed 1844.

Peper Harow, Surrey. Works for Lord Midleton. Begun in 1841 and continued to 1848. Pugin built a gatehouse, a cowfold, a barn, a springhouse, a bridge at Oxenford Farm, where he restored a ruin in the garden and rebuilt the rear of the farmhouse and its chimneys. He also carried out extensive renovations and restorations at Mousehill House, on the Peper Harow estate; the entrance to the house is his and so is the fireplace in the main living room.

Pontefract, Yorkshire. Ackworth Grange. The Jesus Chapel. A private chapel for the Tempest family resident at the Grange. Begun 1841. The entrance hall of the house has some excellent Pugin tiles. Gatehouse and priest's house on the estate resemble Pugin's work but are by Matthew Hadfield. (The chapel is now demolished.)

Princethorpe College, Warwickshire. Pugin added a large window in the end of the old chapel. Drawings dated 1842 show the tracery.

Shepshed, Leicestershire. St Winifride's. (Now abandoned.) Pugin also built a school to accompany this little church. 1842.

Southampton, Hampshire. St Joseph's. 1841–2. (Only the chancel remains.)

Spetchley, Worcestershire. School. 1841.

Stockton-on-Tees, Durham. St Mary's. Ground staked out in May 1841.

Sydney, Australia. Designs for a church sent to Sydney. 1842.

Waterford, Eire. Convent of the Presentation. Drawings prepared in 1841, foundation stone laid in 1842, further designs prepared 1845. E. W. Pugin designed the elaborate fireplace in the parlour and continued to work on the last details of the building after 1852. Additions to the house of Mr Wyse nearby are probably contemporary with the work on the convent.

And in addition Pugin continued to work at Scarisbrick Hall; St Chad's, Birmingham; St George's, Southwark; St Giles', Cheadle; Ushaw College; Oscott College; Alton Towers and Alton; St Wilfrid's, Hulme.
He also produced designs for stained glass, metalwork, carving, sculpture in stone, tiles, textiles and vestments.

202

1843–1844

Albury, Surrey. Albury, Albury House and SS Peter and Paul, Albury Park. Pugin began to work for Henry Drummond, Esq. in 1842–3. He continued to do so until 1851. Then E. W. Pugin undertook the work. The brick chimneys of Albury are Pugin's. 1846–7 he decorated the chapel where Mr Drummond is entombed in the church of SS Peter and Paul. Drawings by Pugin with the measurements of the chapel carefully indicated suggest that he was noting the sizes of an existing building for the purposes of planning the decorative work. Brasses, tiles, sculpture, stained glass, screens, wall painting are all by Pugin. He began to redesign the exterior of Albury House in 1848–9, but in the end the project was largely the work of E. W. Pugin.

Alton, Staffordshire. Alton Castle now St John's Preparatory School for Boys. Foundations laid 1844. Built for the Earl of Shrewsbury. Large chapel, no elaborate formal rooms, remarkable kitchens in the rock beneath the building. Built to be a residence for priests, which explains the institutional character of the interior.

Barntown, Wexford, Eire. St Alphonsus'. Foundation stone 1844. First Mass 1848. Screen has been removed, some of the original glass replaced.

Bishopstone, Wiltshire. St John Baptist. Tomb of the Reverend George Augustus Montgomery, 1844. Montgomery was killed when an arch fell on him in the church being built by Benjamin Ferrey at East Grafton. Details at Bishopstone seem to be by Pugin, among them the piscina and the carving of the vaults in the transept where the tomb stands. The window above the tomb is by Pugin, made by Wailes; it was designed after a medieval window that had been in a church in York until the 1840s.

Blithfield, Staffordshire. Pugin was working for the Honourable and Reverend H. Bagot in 1844. The restoration of the chancel and glass of the east window and the pulpit of St Leonard's, Blithfield, are attributed to Pugin, 1846–51. The parish church, All Saints, Leigh Church, Staffordshire, is not by Pugin but a drawing by him of the floor of the chancel is explained by a remark in a letter that he designed the floor tiles. The connection with Bagot in 1844 may therefore have related to Leigh Church.

Brigg, Lincolnshire. There are numerous references to metalwork orders for Brigg in 1844.

Danesfield, Berkshire. For Mr Scott-Murray, a private chapel. Negotiations for the work begun 1844.

Enniscorthy, Eire. St Aidan's Cathedral. Foundation stone, 1843; Mass first celebrated in partially finished building 1846; nave under construction 1848; tower built 1850, spire completed after Pugin's death, and not from his design. Decoration of the sanctuary J.J. McCarthy.

King's Lynn, Norfolk. St Mary's. Drawings for fittings and tiles for St Mary's 1844. The account with Wailes for the glass 1845. (Now replaced by another building.)

Oxford. Balliol College. Drawings for a new college rejected by the President and Fellows. 1843.
   Magdalen College. A gateway which was widely illustrated and commented upon, designs for a smaller gateway and various other projects – a school for choristers which was not built being the largest – which came Pugin's way because of his friendship with J.R. Bloxham. Gateway 1843–4.

Liverpool. St. Oswald's. Addition of a chapel and school. 1844.

London. Houses of Parliament. In 1844 Pugin renewed his association with Charles Barry and began to design the decorative details for the House of Lords. The relationship with Barry continued until 1852.

Northampton. Cathedral of Our Lady and St Thomas. Pugin church begun 1844 and continued until 1851. It was a simple stone building, cruciform in plan, which has completely disappeared in the course of several building programmes.

Ramsgate, Kent. The Grange. Pugin's own house. A tablet set into the exterior, south chimney, states that it was begun in 1843.

Ratcliffe-on-the-Wreake, Leicestershire. Ratcliffe College. Main front and general plan for the college by Pugin, 1843–4. Building completed by J. Hansom and E.W. Pugin.

Wimborne, Stapehill, Dorset. Holy Cross Abbey. The building is by Charles Hansom. Late 1844, a cross in the cemetery, a memorial to the Reverend Mother Augustin de Chabannes, designed by Pugin.

Wymswold, Leicestershire. St Mary's. Rebuilding and restoration of the church including a Pugin north porch, new glass, a screen, furniture, coronae, pulpit, candlesticks, 1844–50.

In this period Pugin continued a number of major and minor projects he had earlier begun, and supplied a large number of drawings for the decorative arts.

1845–1846

Chirk, Denbighshire. The girls' school at Chirk, 1844–5 is attributed to Pugin. Additions to it appear to be by E.W. Pugin. In 1846 Pugin was 'fitting up' Chirk Castle, where in 1845–7 John Crace and Pugin did work which

cost £2650, and included substantial renovation of the interior on the east side of the castle, a corridor on the courtyard, restoration of the east exterior. E.W. Pugin worked at Chirk in 1854, when he appears to have added outbuildings on the south side of the castle.

Cotton, Staffordshire. Cotton College. St Wilfrid's. Foundation stone October 1844. Ecclesiastical metalwork orders placed with Hardman 1846–9.

Guernsey. St Peter Port. St Joseph's. Designed 1845–6, under construction 1848, completed 1851. The spire was added much later by P.P. Pugin and S.P. Pugin.

Liverpool. Bishop Eton. Our Lady of the Annunciation, 1845–50. Now much added to and altered, but an etching of Pugin's shows that the tower is his and that as he designed it the church had a single transept chapel off a simple nave and chancel. The gate on the street is by Pugin.

Oswaldcroft, house of Mr Sharples, now the Poor Sisters of Nazareth, Home for Incurables. Begun 1844–5, furniture accounts 1847, furniture designs in the Myers papers 1847, glass by Wailes. Painted ceilings, rich fireplaces remain in the house. A small but pretty gatehouse.

Marlow, Buckinghamshire. St Peter's. Foundation stone 1845. Opened 1848. Gate and cross in churchyard by Pugin and a full complement of his decorations. The school and schoolmaster's house are probably by E. W. Pugin, who continued to work at Marlow in 1854.

Maynooth, Eire. St Patrick's College. Pugin began work at Maynooth in 1845–6, and he continued to work there until his death in 1852. The chapel is not his but J. J. McCarthy's.

Midleton, Eire. There are references to work done, houses designed, for Lord Midleton on his Irish estates. Drawings would indicate the work to have been done in 1845.

Nottingham. Convent of Mercy. Drawings prepared 1845. Building not completed until 1850. Furniture and chapel fittings by Pugin.

Rampisham, Dorset. Glebe Farm, school, and restoration of the chancel of the parish church, 1845–6. Altars, glass, font, metalwork by Pugin.

Ramsgate, Kent. St Augustine's. The stone for the church arrived in Ramsgate in December 1845.

Rugby, Warwickshire. St Marie's. Designed 1845–6, opened 1847, much added to by E. W. Pugin and the Reverend Bernard Whelan. Full complement of Pugin decorations and metalwork at the time of the opening.

Tagoat, Eire. Parish church. Metalwork order sent to Tagoat in 1845, church opened in 1846. Additions in the east.

Totnes, Devonshire. Dartington Hall. In 1845, at the request of Mr Champernoune, Pugin prepared drawings for additions and restorations at Dartington Hall. The style he chose resembled his drawings for Balliol College of 1843. The work was never carried out. The drawings are extant.

Tubney, Berkshire. St Lawrence. The church, rectory and school all by Pugin 1845–7. The interior of the church is notable for the design of the font and the decoration of the chancel.

Ware, Hertfordshire. St Edmund's College. Pugin worked at the college from 1846 until his death. The chapel is a particularly good example of his late style; remarkable stone screen, altar and reredos. The house, now St Hugh's school, is by Pugin, 1851.

West Tofts, Norfolk. St Mary's. (Now not in use as a church; it is in the Battle School area.) Many sheets of drawings for the furnishing and architecture of this church. The organ is now at South Pickenham, nearby.

Woodchester Park, near Stroud, Gloucestershire. 1845–6. Pugin was working for Mr Leigh, for whom he designed a house, never built. Negotiations for a church and monastery at the edge of the estate fell through and Charles Hansom was given the commission. Drawings for both projects have survived.

In addition Pugin produced the drawings for the decorations of the Houses of Parliament, supervised and continued to produce drawings for the buildings being completed from his designs, supplied J. Crace with designs for wallpapers, furniture, and the interiors of houses, produced the cartoons for the stained glass windows and the designs for metalwork which J. Hardman required.

1847–1848

Adare, Eire. Adare Manor. Built for and by the Second Earl of Dunraven. Details in the hall, various fireplaces, general design of the dining hall taken from the A. W. Pugin drawings which are in the collection at Adare Manor. Drawings dated 1846–7. In addition Pugin added a new roof and stained glass windows to the village church, which he probably also totally restored.

Bakewell, Derbyshire. Burton Closes. Pugin seems to have been called in when the house was partially built, for when he first refers to it he says he has taken on the 'job of fitting up a large house near Haddon'. He decorated and completed the whole interior, and he certainly added a side entrance and the passage leading to it. The

staircase hall is a good example of his decoration, and may have been entirely designed by him. Pugin visited the house 1847–8 and the orders for metal-work for it are of the same date. In 1854 E. W. Pugin was working there.

Birr, Eire. Convent. Foundation stone laid 1846 but the first portions were not built until 1847. In 1848 an illustration of his scheme for the building appeared in the *Irish Catholic Directory*. Building largely completed by E. W. Pugin. Chapel has been greatly revised.

Blackmore Park, Worcestershire Our Blessed Lady and St Alphonsus. Designed by Charles Hansom and opened in 1847, the metalwork is all by Pugin, and constitutes a fine display.

Erdington, Warwickshire. SS Thomas and Edmund of Canterbury. Erdington Abbey. Architect Charles Hansom for the Reverend Daniel Haigh. A complete and especially rich collection of Pugin vestments, stained glass and metalwork. 1848–50. The small school building by Pugin which stood nearby has been demolished.

Hornby Castle, Yorkshire. Pugin was paid £200 in 1847 for designs which he prepared for the Duke of Leeds.

Lanteglos-by-Camelford, Cornwall. Rectory. Pugin supplied the plans but no supervision of the building process. 1847. (Additions have been made to it recently.)

Lincoln. St Anne's Bedehouses. Built by Myers from Pugin's designs but without his advice or supervision. 1847.

London. Westminster. The Church of the Immaculate Conception. Farm Street. The high altar and its fittings were designed by Pugin in 1848 at the order of Miss Monica Tempest.

Fulham. St Thomas of Canterbury. Church and presbytery by Pugin. 1847-9. High altar, reredos of the Lady Chapel, font and pulpit all carved in Caen stone to Pugin designs.

Milton Abbey, Dorset. Designs 1847-8 for extensive building and decorative schemes including stained glass for which the estimate was £3900. Lord Portarlington was unable to carry out the scheme because of the failure of his Irish rents.

Salisbury, Wiltshire. St Osmund. At first a simple church comparable to Pugin's least elaborate. 1847-9. Nave and north aisle have been added. The altar in the south chapel is by Pugin.

Tetbury, Gloucestershire. St Saviour. Hardman and Pugin carried out the painting and gilding of the ceiling and reredos, in the chancel. 1848.

Wilburton, Cambridgeshire. Manor House, now Manor School. Attributed to Pugin, whose work it resembles on the exterior and in its plan. 1848. That Pugin was indeed in Wilburton in 1848 seems likely because a drawing survives for the chancel seating of Wilburton Church. It is dated 1848.

Winwick, Lancashire. St Oswald. Pugin rebuilt the chancel of this church in 1847-9.

And Pugin continued with his work for the Houses of Parliament, made a major addition to Alton Towers, completed St Augustine's Ramsgate, supplied Crace, Hardman, and Myers with designs, continued to work at Ushaw College and others of his buildings which were not yet completed.

1849–1850

Bicton. Bicton Grange, Devonshire. The Rolle mortuary chapel. 1850, Lady Rolle received permission to take down the old church. Chapel, and all its decoration by Pugin. Tomb of Lord Rolle from Myers workshop. 1850.

Birmingham. Aston. Chapel standing in cemetery. A. W. Pugin chancel and chapel, the rest E. W. Pugin. 1850.

Cambridge. Jesus College Chapel. Redecoration of the chapel, 1849–52, and continued from his designs after his death.

207

Ledbury, Herefordshire. Eastnor Castle. Crace and Pugin decorated the drawing room. Drawings by Pugin are dated 1849.

Hastings, Sussex. Convent of the Christ Jesus, St Leonard's. Chapel said to have been begun by Pugin. There is no reference to this building in the Pugin documents.

Lismore, Eire. Lismore Castle. The Sixth Duke of Devonshire was the client of Crace rather than Pugin. 1849–50 decorations. Pugin never visited the building.

London. St George's, Southwark. The Petre Chantry. 1850.

Sheffield. St Marie's, architect Matthew Hadfield. There are Pugin designs for the reredos and high altar, 1849–51, but those presently in the church do not match the Pugin drawings.

Welshpool, Montgomeryshire. Leighton Hall. Decorations supervised by Crace; Pugin never visited the house. 1850.

And Pugin completed St Augustine's, Ramsgate in 1850. Continued his work with Crace and Hardman, provided drawings for Charles Barry.

1851–1852

London. Greenwich. Our Lady Star of the Sea. The architect of the church was Wardell but Pugin

208

designed the decoration of the chancel and the chapel of St Joseph. 1851. His decorations are still in the church.

Pantasaph, Flintshire. St David's. Pugin was called in to assist with the arrangement of the church; its architect was Thomas Wyatt, its patron Lord Feilding. This was one of the last responsibilities of Pugin's life, and only after his death did the flood of orders for its metalwork reach J. Hardman. 1850–1.

With the exception of architectural and decorative assignments he had accepted and was continuing, the work at Greenwich and Pantasaph were the only new orders Pugin received in 1851.

ADDITIONAL
INFORMATION

Bolton Abbey, Yorkshire. The south windows at Bolton Abbey carry the following inscription: 'These windows were ordered by William Spencer, Duke of Devonshire, John G. Crace fecit 1853.' The windows were designed under the supervision of Pugin.

Yarmouth, Norfolk. There are drawings, undated, for an elaborately carved pulpit which Pugin entitled 'pulpit for Yarmouth'.

Prescot, Lancashire. Our Lady Immaculate and St Joseph. There is a Pugin drawing for the seating in the sanctuary and for the screen of this church.

Thurnham, Lancashire. SS Thomas and Elizabeth. The church is not by Pugin but there are two sheets of drawings for the screen of the Lady Chapel and a large order of metal-work fittings. The altar appears in the Hardman records. The latter is dated 1848.

Bellevue, Wexford, Eire. The private chapel for the Cliffe family, sometimes attributed to Pugin, is not by him but by McCarthy.

Birtley, Durham. St Joseph's. Though this church has long been attributed to Pugin it is not his.

Salt, Staffordshire. The screen from the Alton Towers chapel is now in the parish church at Salt.

Boston, Lincolnshire. St Botolph. The font given to the church by Beresford Hope in 1853 is surely by E. W. Pugin rather than A. W. Pugin. It should be compared with the design of the chapel of St Aloysius at Ushaw College.

Castle Rock, Leicestershire. Attributed to Pugin and dated c. 1840. There is little about this house to confirm such an attribution.

Bilston, Staffordshire. Holy Trinity.

There is a Pugin drawing for the chancel of this church.

Dewsbury, Yorkshire. Our Lady and St Paulinus has been attributed to A. W. Pugin. The documents at the church indicate that E. W. Pugin was the architect but it seems clear that he followed his father's two drawings, 1838, for Dudley church in making his design.

Edermine, near Enniscorthy, Eire. A private chapel has been attributed to Pugin. The window of the chapel is exactly like various drawings in the early Pugin notebooks.

Cobh, Eire. In 1842 Pugin mentions two villas he was designing for Lord Midleton at Cobh.

Little Horsted, Sussex. Horsted Place. In his last years Pugin was unable to keep Myers busy with contracts. Horsted Place seems to have been built by Myers, with the assistance of the men usually associated with Pugin. There is no mention of the house in the Pugin documents.

Necton, Norfolk. All Saints. A monument to Col Mason in the church has been attributed to Pugin and dated 1835. The only mention of the Masons or Necton in the Pugin documents occurs in 1850.

Unless they are mentioned in the list below all the illustrations are from photographs by the author.

Bibliography

Books and pamphlets by A. W. Pugin, in chronological order:

Gothic Furniture in the Style of the 15th Century designed and etched by A. W. N. Pugin (London: Ackermann and Co., 1835)

A Letter to A. W. Hakewill, Architect, in answer to his reflections on the style for rebuilding the Houses of Parliament (Salisbury: for the author, 1835)

The History and Antiquities of the Vicar's Close, Wells . . . consisting of plans, elevations, sections and parts at large . . . by A. W. Pugin . . . under the direction of the late Augustus Pugin . . . accompanied by historical and descriptive accounts by Thomas Larkin Walker (London: printed for the author, 1836; being series 3, part 1 of *Examples of Gothic Architecture*)

Designs for Gold and Silversmiths (London: Ackermann and Co., 1836)

Designs for Iron and Brass Work in the style of the XV and XVI centuries, drawn and etched by A. W. N. Pugin (London: Ackermann and Co., 1836)

Contrasts; or, A Parallel Between the Noble Edifices of the Fourteenth and Fifteenth Centuries, and Similar Buildings of the Present Day; shewing the Present Decay of Taste: Accompanied by appropriate Text (Salisbury: for the author, 1836; a second and much revised edition, London: Dolman, 1841; the second edition in facsimile reprint, with the one plate from the 1836 edition which Pugin omitted from the second edition included and an introduction by Henry-Russell Hitchcock, Leicester, 1969)

Details of antient houses of the 15th and 16th centuries selected from those existing at Rouen+ Caen+ Beauvais+ Gisors+ Abbeville+ Strasbourg+ etc, drawn on the spot and etched by A. Welby Pugin (London: Ackermann, 1836)

A Reply to Observations which Appeared in 'Fraser's Magazine', for March, 1837, on a Work Entitled 'Contrasts', by the author of that Publication (London: the author, 1837)

An Apology for a work entitled 'Contrasts'; being a defence of the assertions advanced in that publication, against the various attacks lately made upon it. By A. Welby Pugin, Author of the Book in Question (Birmingham: R. P. Stone, 1837)

A Letter on the Proposed Protestant Memorial to Cranmer, Ridley, and Latymer, Addressed to the subscribers to and Promoters of That Undertaking (London: Booker and Dolman, 1839)

The True Principles of Pointed or Christian Architecture: set forth in two Lectures delivered at St Marie's, Oscott, by A. Welby Pugin, Architect, and Professor of Ecclesiastical Antiquities in that College (London: John Weale, 1841)

The Present State of Ecclesiastical Architecture in England with Thirty-Six Illustrations, republished from *The Dublin Review* (London: Charles Dolman, 1843)

An Apology for The Revival of Christian Architecture in England (London: John Weale, 1843)

Glossary of Ecclesiastical Ornament and Costume, compiled and illustrated from antient authorities and examples with Extracts from the Works of Durandus, Georgius, Bona, Catalani, Gerbert, Martene, Molanus, Theirs, Mabillon, Ducange, etc. Faithfully Translated by the Rev. Bernard Smith, of St Marie's College, Oscott (London: Bohn, 1844, 1846, 1868)

Sutton, John and Pugin, A. W. *A short Account of Organs Built in England from the Reign of King Charles the Second to the present time* (London: Masters, 1847)

Floriated Ornament: a series of thirty-one designs (London: Bohn, 1849)

The Present State of Public Worship among the Roman Catholics, By a Roman Catholic (London, 1850)

An Address to the Inhabitants of Ramsgate (Ramsgate, 1850)

An Earnest Appeal for the Revival of Ancient Plain Song (London: Dolman, 1850)

Copy of a Letter addressed to the Editor of 'The Tablet' Newspaper (n.p., n.d., but probably 1851)

A Treatise on Chancel Screens and Rood Lofts, their antiquity, use, and symbolic signification (London, 1851)

Some Remarks on the Articles Which Have Recently Appeared in the 'Rambler', Relative to Ecclesiastical Architecture and Decoration (London: Dolman, 1851)

An Earnest Address on the Subject of the Re-establishment of the Hierarchy (London: Dolman, 1851)

In addition Pugin contributed to *The Tablet, The Catholic Weekly Instructor, The Catholic Magazine, The Orthodox Journal*

Books and articles relevant to Pugin, his works, and his times:

Photographs from Sketches by A. W. N. Pugin, ed. E. W. Pugin (London: S. Ayling, 1865)

BOASE, T. S. R., *English Art, 1800–1870* (London: Oxford University Press, 1959)

BOGAN, THE REVEREND BERNARD, *The Great Link, A History of St George's, Southwark, 1786–1848* (London: Burns and Oates, 1848)

BURY, SHIRLEY, *Copy or Creation, Victorian Treasures from English Churches*, Catalogue of an exhibition organized by the Worshipful Company of Goldsmiths and the Victorian Society. Foreword by Sir John Betjeman (London: 1967)
    'In Search of Pugin's Church Plate', *Connoisseur*, CLXV, May 1967
    'Pugin's Marriage Jewellery', *Victoria and Albert Museum Yearbook*, 1969

BURY, TALBOT, Editorial and leading article, an obituary of A. W. Pugin, *The Builder*, September 1852

CLARK, KENNETH, *The Gothic Revival* (London: Constable, 1928, and Penguin, 1962)

211

EASTLAKE, CHARLES, *A History of the Gothic Revival* (London, 1872)

FERREY, BENJAMIN, *Recollections of A.N. Welby Pugin and his Father Augustus Pugin* (London: Stanford, 1861)

FERRIDAY, PETER, ed., *Victorian Architecture* (London: Jonathan Cape, 1963)

GWYNN, DENIS R., *Lord Shrewsbury, Pugin and the Catholic Revival* (London: Hollis and Carter, 1946)

HITCHCOCK, HENRY-RUSSELL, *Early Victorian Architecture in Britain*, 2 vols (New Haven: Yale, 1954)
    Architecture, Nineteenth and Twentieth Centuries (London: Penguin, 1958)

HOUGHTON, WALTER E., *The Victorian Frame of Mind* (New Haven and London: Yale and Oxford University Press, 1957)

MILBURN, THE VERY REVEREND DAVID, *A History of Ushaw College* (Ushaw: The Ushaw Bookshop, 1964)

PEVSNER, SIR NIKOLAUS, *The Buildings of England*, vols 1ff
    'A short Pugin florilegium', *Architectural Review*, 94: 31–4, August 1943

PIPER, JOHN, 'St Marie's Grange: The first home of A. W. N. Pugin', *Architectural Review*, 98: 90–3, March 1945

PORT, M.H., *Six Hundred New Churches* (London: SPCK, 1961)

PURCELL, EDMUND SHERIDAN, *Ambrose Phillipps de Lisle*, 2 vols (London: Macmillan, 1900)

ROPE, HENRY E.G., *Pugin* (Ditchling: Pepler and Sewell, 1935)

SIRR, HARRY E.G., 'Augustus Welby Pugin; a sketch', *Journal of the Royal Institute of British Architects*, August 1918

STANTON, PHOEBE B., *The Gothic Revival and American Church Architecture, An Episode in Taste, 1840–1856* (Baltimore: The Johns Hopkins Press, 1968)
    'Pugin at Twenty-one', *Architectural Review*, 110: 187–90, September 1951
    'Some Comments on the Life and Works of Augustus Welby Northmore Pugin', *Journal of the Royal Institute of British Architects*, December 1952
    'Pugin: Principles of Design versus Revivalism', *Journal of the Society of Architectural Historians*, December 1954
    'The Sources of Pugin's *Contrasts*', in *Concerning Architecture*, editor Sir John Summerson (London: Allen Lane the Penguin Press, 1968)

SUMMERSON, SIR JOHN, 'Pugin at Ramsgate', *Architectural Review*, April 1948

TRAPPES-LOMAX, MICHAEL, *Pugin, A Medieval Victorian* (London: Sheed and Ward, 1932)

WATERHOUSE, PAUL, 'Life and Work of Welby Pugin,' *Architectural Review*, iii, 1894, Parts 1, 2, 3, iv; 1895, Parts 4, 5, 6, 7

WHITE, JAMES E., *The Cambridge Movement, the Ecclesiologists and the Gothic Revival* (Cambridge: the University Press, 1962)

WILLIAMS, RAYMOND, *Culture and Society, 1780–1950* (London and New York: Chatto and Windus and Columbia University Press, 1958, and Harper and Row, 1966)

Index

References in italics are to illustrations

215